Table of Contents

0-7696-4038-9 *Problem Solving*

Introduction

The activities in *Using the Standards—Problem Solving* were developed in accordance with standards as prescribed by the National Council of Teachers of Mathematics (NCTM), with a focus on problem solving. Students will build new mathematical knowledge, solve problems in context, apply and adapt appropriate strategies, and reflect on the problem-solving process. The content is divided by the NCTM content standards:

Number and Operations: Understand numbers, ways of representing numbers, relationships among numbers, and number systems. Understand meanings of operations and how they relate to one another. Compute fluently and make reasonable estimates.

Algebra: Understand patterns, relations, and functions. Represent and analyze mathematical situations and structures using algebraic symbols. Use mathematical models to represent and understand quantitative relationships. Analyze change in various contexts.

Geometry: Analyze characteristics and properties of two- and three-dimensional geometric shapes and develop mathematical arguments about geometric relationships. Specify locations and describe spatial relationships using coordinate geometry and other representational systems. Apply transformations and use symmetry to analyze mathematical situations. Use visualization, spatial reasoning, and geometric modeling to solve problems.

Measurement: Understand measurable attributes of objects and the units, systems, and processes of measurement. Apply appropriate techniques, tools, and formulas to determine measurements.

Data Analysis and Probability: Formulate questions that can be addressed with data and collect, organize, and display relevant data to answer them. Select and use appropriate statistical methods to analyze data. Develop and evaluate inferences and predictions that are based on data. Understand and apply basic concepts of probability.

Within each content section, the activities also incorporate the NCTM process standards. These strands focus on the mathematical processes that students draw on to acquire and use their content knowledge. Student pages are marked with the following icons to assist in identifying the five process standards for mathematics. An NCTM Standards Correlation Chart is also provided on page 6 for a listing of page numbers by process strand.

Using the Standards
Problem Solving

Grade 8

Published by Milestone
an imprint of
Frank Schaffer Publications®

Editors: Krista Fanning, Melissa Warner Hale
Cover Artist: Lori Kibbey

Frank Schaffer Publications®

Milestone is an imprint of Frank Schaffer Publications.

Send all inquiries to:
Frank Schaffer Publications
3195 Wilson Drive NW
Grand Rapids, Michigan 49534

Using the Standards: Problem Solving—grade 8

ISBN: 0-7696-4038-9

3 4 5 6 7 8 9 10 PAT 10 09 08 07 06

Introduction (cont.)

Problem Solving: Build new mathematical knowledge through problem solving. Solve problems that arise in mathematics and in other contexts. Apply and adapt a variety of appropriate strategies to solve problems. Monitor and reflect on the process of mathematical problem solving.

Reasoning and Proof: Recognize reasoning and proof as fundamental aspects of mathematics. Make and investigate mathematical conjectures. Develop and evaluate mathematical arguments and proofs. Select and use various types of reasoning and methods of proof.

Communication: Organize and consolidate mathematical thinking through communication. Communicate mathematical thinking coherently and clearly to peers, teachers, and others. Analyze and evaluate the mathematical thinking and strategies of others. Use the language of mathematics to express ideas precisely.

Connections: Recognize and use connections among mathematical ideas. Understand how those ideas interconnect and build on one another to produce a coherent whole. Recognize and apply mathematics in contexts outside of mathematics.

Representation: Create and use representations to organize, record, and communicate mathematical ideas. Select, apply, and translate among mathematical representations to solve problems. Use representations to model and interpret physical, social, and mathematical situations.

These activities can be done independently, in pairs, or in groups. Problems may be broken into parts, with class discussion following student work. Many activities will lead into subjects that can be investigated or discussed further as a class. Students may compare different solution methods or discuss how to select a valid solution method for a particular problem.

Each section ends with a **Check Your Skills** page. These activities provide a representative sampling of all types of processes and skills developed throughout each content section. This activity can be used as additional practice or as a posttest.

A **Pretest** and **Cumulative Assessment** are also provided as an integral part of the learning process. Other assessments may include observations, conversations, interviews, interactive journals, writing prompts, and independent quizzes or tests. Classroom discussions help students learn the difference between poor, good, and excellent responses.

NCTM Standards Correlation Chart

	Reasoning and Proof	Communication	Connections	Representation
Number and Operations	10, 11, 12, 14, 15, 16, 17, 22, 29	9, 10, 11, 14, 15, 19, 20, 25, 28, 30	14, 15, 23, 24, 25, 26, 27, 28, 29, 30	13, 18, 19, 20, 21, 23, 24
Algebra	32, 33, 34, 35, 42, 43	34, 35, 36, 37, 43, 45, 46, 53, 55	32, 33, 34, 35, 39, 40, 41, 47, 48, 49	36, 37, 38, 39, 40, 41, 42, 44, 45, 46, 47, 50, 51, 52, 53, 54, 55
Geometry	63, 64, 68, 73, 74, 77, 78	58, 59, 61, 72, 75	57, 62, 63, 64, 65, 66, 67, 68, 69, 70, 71	57, 58, 59, 60, 61, 62, 63, 64, 69, 70, 71, 72, 76, 79, 80
Measurement	82, 83, 84, 85, 86, 89, 90, 91, 92	91, 92	84, 85, 86, 88, 89, 90, 91, 92, 93	87, 88
Data Analysis and Probability	98, 100	96, 98, 99, 101, 102	95, 96, 97, 98, 99, 100, 101, 102, 103, 104, 106, 107	95, 96, 97, 99, 101, 102, 105, 106, 107

*All pages are problem solving, so the Problem Solving icon does not appear on the pages or in this chart.

**The Pretest, Check Your Skills, and Cumulative Assessment pages are not included in this chart, but they do contain a representative sampling of all content and process standards.

Name ______________________ Date ___________

Pretest

1. Explain how $(^-2)^3$ and $(2)^{-3}$ are related.

2. Write the following two numbers in scientific notation.

a. 89,400,000,000 ______________ **b.** 0.0000065 ______________

3. Simplify the expression below. Explain how you know which steps to do first.

$(^-16 + 20)^2 + 6 \div (\sqrt[3]{8}) =$ ________

4. The marketing department in a tennis shoe company is expecting to boost sales 175% in the next year. This year the company sold 230,000,000 pairs of tennis shoes. How many pairs of shoes does the company have to sell next year to meet its goal?

5. Look at the following sequence. Figure out the pattern. Write in the missing numbers. Explain what strategy you used to find the pattern.

1, 4, $^-1$, 6, $^-3$, ____, $^-5$, 10, $^-7$, 12, $^-9$, 14, $^-11$, 16, $^-13$, ____, ____, ____, $^-17$

6. Write an equivalent math statement for each equation.

Twice x is 4 more than y. ____

$2y + x = 6$ ____

7. Marcus is building a triangular tool shed with the dimensions below. Explain to Marcus whether his plans will work. Give two reasons to support your answer.

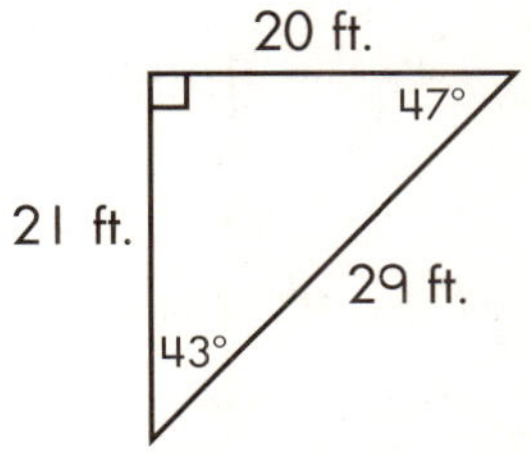

0-7696-4038-9 *Problem Solving*

Name ______________________ Date __________

Pretest (cont.)

8. On this circle identify a tangent, radius, chord, semicircle, and minor arc. Use each term's definition to support your answers.

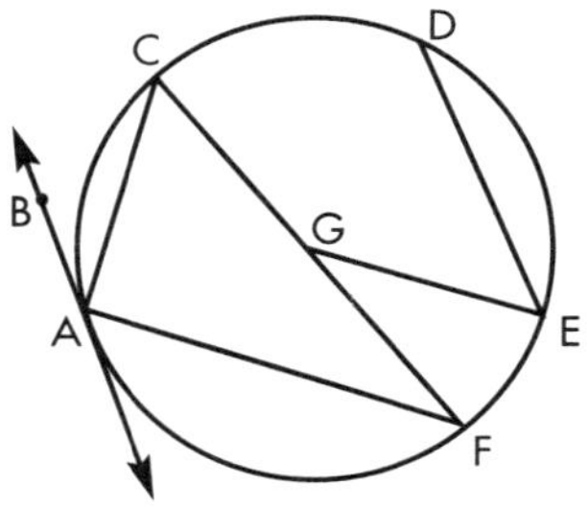

9. Find the perimeter and area of the following curved shape. Include the appropriate units in your answer. Show all of your work.

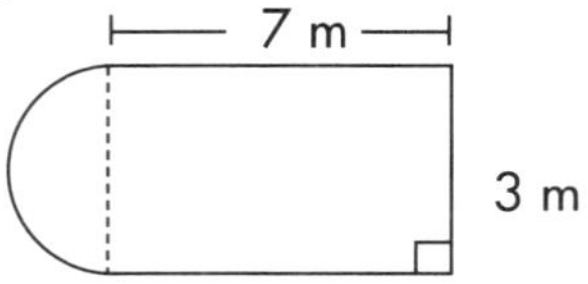

10. Compare the surface area and volume for the following rectangular prism. Which one is the larger measurement?

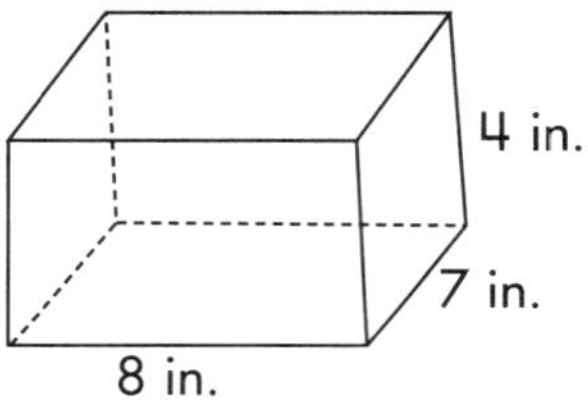

11. Treyvon can climb a rope at a rate of 374 cm/10 sec. How many meters per minute is this? Explain how you arrived at your answer.

12. Give a set of six data values that have the following measurements.

Mean: 25
Median: 25
Mode: 10 and 30
Range: 40

Data set: ______________________

13. On the spinner at the right, find the probability for each outcome below.

P(7) = __________

P(number > 2) = __________

P(odd number) = __________

P(not 5) = __________

P(factor of 60) = __________

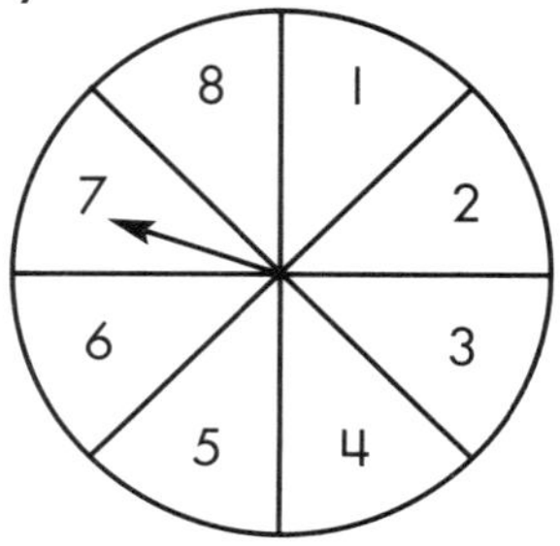

Name ______________________ Date ____________

Types of Numbers

A **prime number** is a number that has exactly two factors, 1 and itself.
A **composite number** is a number that has more than two factors.

A whole number is **abundant** if the sum of all of its factors (not including itself) is more than the number.
Example: 24. Its factors are 1, 2, 3, 4, 6, and 12. The sum of these is 28. This is greater than 24, so 24 is an abundant number.

A whole number is **deficient** if the sum of all of its factors (not including itself) is less than the number.
Example: 15. Its factors are 1, 3, and 5. The sum of these is 9. This is less than 15, so 15 is a deficient number.

A whole number is **perfect** if the sum of all of its factors (not including itself) is equal to the number.

Directions: Using the above definitions, find examples of these types of numbers.

1. Consider the numbers 1 to 30.

- **a.** Make a list of abundant numbers in this range.
- **b.** What properties do the abundant numbers have in common?
- **c.** Predict the next three abundant numbers above 30.

2. Make a list of deficient numbers from 1 to 30.

3. Are there any perfect numbers between 1 and 30? List them.

4. Consider the numbers 1 to 50.

- **a.** Make a list of all of the prime numbers.
- **b.** Are the rest of the numbers in this range composite?

0-7696-4038-9 *Problem Solving*

Name ______________________ Date ___________

Number Explorations

Directions: Use your number knowledge for each exploratory situation. Show all of your work and reasoning.

1. Treyvon tells his math partners that he's made a discovery. He says that every whole number greater than 1 can be written as a product of *only* prime numbers. For example, he shows that 18 can be written as 2 x 3 x 3, that 40 can be written as 2 x 2 x 2 x 5, and so on. Is Treyvon correct? To arrive at your answer, test at least 10 numbers, including two 3-digit, two 4-digit, two 5-digit, two 6-digit, and two 7-digit numbers.

2. Lui has a theory about 2-digit numbers that have a larger tens digit than ones digit. She says that reversing the digits and subtracting the reversed number from the original number will *always* generate a number that is a multiple of 9. Is Lui right? If so, why do you think this works? If not, why not?

Would the same pattern work for 3-digit numbers in which the hundreds digit is larger than the tens digit and the tens digit is larger than the ones digit? Would the same pattern work for 4-digit numbers?

3. Alicia announces to her class that she's discovered a method to detect whether a number is a perfect square. If the sum of its digits is either 9 or 18, she says the number has to be a perfect square. As evidence, she shows the class the numbers 9, 81, 144, and 234. Is Alicia correct? Do your own research and support your conclusion with words and numerical evidence.

Name ______________________ Date ___________

Number Explorations (cont.)

4. Make a table showing the first 20 perfect square numbers. Note any patterns and similarities you find. Then try to predict whether the following numbers are perfect squares:

15,625 529 798 4,624

Explain your reasoning, basing your explanation on the table you made. Use a calculator to check your answer.

5. Rank the following numbers in order from largest to smallest. First, try to rank them without using a calculator or pencil and paper. Next, estimate the difference between each of the numbers in your ranking and explain the basis of your estimates. Finally, use a calculator to check your estimates by finding the numbers' exact values.

2^{10} 11^5 13^3 8,000 8^7 5^4 200,000 5×10^4 9^6

6. Begin by converting some common fractions to decimals. Find five fractions with different denominators that become repeating decimals when converted to decimal form. Repeating decimals end in a repeating number or pattern of numbers. Look at your fractions and try to establish some rules for detecting whether a fraction will become a repeating decimal. Then use your rules to predict whether the following fractions will repeat. Check to confirm your predictions.

$\frac{8}{24}$ $\frac{7}{150}$ $\frac{9}{99}$ $\frac{142}{710}$ $\frac{75}{225}$

0-7696-4038-9 *Problem Solving*

Name ______________________ Date __________

Integers and the Commutative Property

Directions: Write the integers in order from least to greatest.

1. 50, 2, ${}^{-}40$, ${}^{-}48$, 39, ${}^{-}10$, 15, ${}^{-}39$

____

2. ${}^{-}3{,}012$, ${}^{-}2{,}891$, ${}^{-}4{,}560$, ${}^{-}3{,}201$, ${}^{-}4{,}559$, ${}^{-}2{,}999$, ${}^{-}3{,}021$, ${}^{-}5{,}472$

____

Write *T* if the number sentence is true. Write *F* if it is false.

3. ${}^{-}5 + 7 = 7 + {}^{-}5$ ________

4. ${}^{-}9 + {}^{-}3 = {}^{-}3 + {}^{-}9$ ________

5. ${}^{-}6 - {}^{-}4 = {}^{-}4 - {}^{-}6$ ________

6. $4 - {}^{-}2 = {}^{-}2 - 4$ ________

7. ${}^{-}31 + 135 = 135 + {}^{-}31$ ________

8. ${}^{-}88 - 22 = 22 - {}^{-}88$ ________

The **commutative property** says the order of the values can be switched without changing the answer.

9. Is addition of integers commutative? That is, does $a + b = b + a$ for all integers a and b? Explain.

10. Is subtraction of integers commutative? That is, does $a - b = b - a$ for all integers a and b? Explain.

11. Try changing the order of the numerals in several multiplication problems with integers. Is multiplication of integers commutative? Explain.

12. Try changing the order of the numerals in several division problems with integers. Is division of integers commutative? Explain.

0-7696-4038-9 *Problem Solving*

Name ______________________ Date ____________

Fractions and the Associative Property

An operation is **associative** if you can change the grouping of the numbers and still get the same result.

Directions: Next to each problem number, write the letter of the expression that gives the same answer. Not all letter choices will be used.

____ **1.** $\left(\frac{1}{3} + \frac{2}{3}\right) + \frac{1}{2}$

____ **2.** $\frac{3}{5} \times \left(\frac{2}{5} \times 8\frac{1}{2}\right)$

____ **3.** $\frac{4}{5} \times \left(1\frac{1}{4} \times \frac{2}{3}\right)$

____ **4.** $\left(\frac{4}{7} + \frac{3}{14}\right) + \frac{5}{21}$

____ **5.** $\left(\frac{5}{6} + \frac{1}{12}\right) + \frac{3}{24}$

____ **6.** $\left(\frac{8}{9} \times \frac{18}{64}\right) \times 1\frac{17}{21}$

A. $\left(\frac{4}{5} \times 1\frac{1}{4}\right) \times \frac{2}{3}$

B. $\frac{8}{9} \times \left(\frac{18}{64} \div 1\frac{7}{21}\right)$

C. $\frac{5}{6} + \left(\frac{1}{12} + \frac{3}{24}\right)$

D. $\frac{8}{9} \times \left(\frac{18}{64} \times 1\frac{17}{21}\right)$

E. $\frac{4}{7} + \left(\frac{3}{14} + \frac{5}{21}\right)$

F. $\frac{3}{5} \div \left(\frac{2}{5} \times 8\frac{1}{2}\right)$

G. $\frac{3}{5} \times \left(\frac{2}{5} \div 8\frac{1}{2}\right)$

H. $\frac{1}{3} + \left(\frac{2}{3} + \frac{1}{2}\right)$

I. $\left(\frac{3}{5} \times \frac{2}{5}\right) \times 8\frac{1}{2}$

Look for patterns in the matching problems above. Then complete these equations, where *a*, *b*, and *c* are fractions.

7. $(a + b) + c =$ ______________________

8. $a \times (b \times c) =$ ______________________

0-7696-4038-9 *Problem Solving*

Name ____________________ Date __________

Using the Properties

Directions: Read each situation to develop your knowledge of mathematical properties.

1. Enrico has an extensive CD collection. He is sorting out his CDs. He arranges them in 6 rows of 15. Then he arranges them into 15 rows of 6.

a. Write an expression to model the first CD arrangement. ____________________

b. Write an expression to model the second CD arrangement. ____________________

c. How are the expressions you wrote in parts **a** and **b** related? How do you know?

____

d. What mathematical property is illustrated by this example? Explain.

2. Alicia has a bag of 100 red jelly beans. She also has a bag of 75 green jelly beans and another bag of 60 green jelly beans.

a. Write an expression that models the total number of jelly beans.

____

b. What if the bag of 75 jelly beans actually had red jelly beans instead of green jelly beans? Write an expression that models the total number of jelly beans.

____

c. How are the expressions you wrote in parts **a** and **b** related? Explain how you know.

d. What mathematical property is illustrated by this example? Explain.

Name ______________________ Date ___________

Using the Properties (cont.)

3. The art teacher is passing out supplies. She has 4 boxes of acrylic paints, each of which contains 8 bottles. She has 4 boxes of water-based paints, each of which contains 10 bottles.

a. Write an expression that models the number of bottles of paint the art teacher has altogether.

____

b. The art teacher evenly distributes all of the paint bottles into 4 new plastic containers. Write a different expression that models the number of bottles of paint the art teacher has altogether.

____

c. How are the expressions you wrote in parts **a** and **b** related? Explain how you know.

d. What mathematical property is illustrated by this example? Explain.

4. Rewrite each expression below in an equivalent form. Next to each expression, write the name of the mathematical property that is being used.

a. 45 x 23 = ______________________ ______________________

b. 17 x (29 + 63) = ______________________ ______________________

c. (86 + 72) + 211 = ______________________ ______________________

d. (7 + 24) x 13 = ______________________ ______________________

e. 3,456 + 8,192 = ______________________ ______________________

f. 27 x 44 − 18 x 44 = ______________________ ______________________

EXPLAINING

Explain the mechanics and uses of the commutative, associative, and distributive properties.

Name ____________________ Date __________

Integers and Exponents

$(^-2)^4$ means "take $^-2$ to the fourth power."
$^-2^4$ means "find the opposite of 2 to the fourth power."

$(^-2)^4 = (^-2) \times (^-2) \times (^-2) \times (^-2)$
$= 4 \times 4 = 16$

$^-2^4 = ^-(2 \times 2 \times 2 \times 2)$
$= ^-(4 \times 4) = ^-16$

Directions: Find the value of each number.

1. $(^-5)^2$

2. $^-3^3$

3. $^-4^2$

4. $(^-3)^2$

5. $^-2^6$

6. $(^-8)^4$

A **negative exponent** means take the reciprocal and then take the power.

$$2^{-3} = (\tfrac{1}{2})^3 = \tfrac{1}{2} \times \tfrac{1}{2} \times \tfrac{1}{2} = \tfrac{1}{8}$$

$$(^-4)^{-3} = (-\tfrac{1}{4})^3 = -\tfrac{1}{4} \times -\tfrac{1}{4} \times -\tfrac{1}{4} = -\tfrac{1}{64}$$

Find the value of each number.

7. 5^{-2}

8. 3^{-3}

9. $(^-5)^{-3}$

10. $(^-2)^{-5}$

11. $(^-3)^{-4}$

12. 6^{-2}

Find the value of the missing number. Explain how you know your answer is correct.

13. $(7)^x = 343$

14. $(x)^{-2} = \frac{1}{16}$

15. $9^x = \frac{1}{6{,}561}$

REFLECTING

If $3^{-2} = \frac{1}{9}$, does 2^{-3} also equal $\frac{1}{9}$?

0-7696-4038-9 *Problem Solving*

Name ______________________ Date ____________

Fractions and Exponents

If the exponent is outside of the parentheses, the entire fraction should be raised to the power.

$$\left(\frac{4}{5}\right)^3 = \frac{4}{5} \times \frac{4}{5} \times \frac{4}{5} = \frac{64}{125}$$

If only a part of the fraction is raised to a power, then only that number is raised to the power.

$$\frac{4^3}{5} = 4 \times 4 \times \frac{4}{5} = \frac{64}{5} = 12\frac{4}{5}$$

A negative exponent means take the reciprocal and then take the power.

$$\left(\frac{4}{5}\right)^{-3} = \left(\frac{5}{4}\right)^3 = \frac{5}{4} \times \frac{5}{4} \times \frac{5}{4} = \frac{125}{64} = 1\frac{61}{64}$$

Directions: Write each of the following fractions in simplest form.

1. $\left(\frac{5}{6}\right)^2$

2. $\left(\frac{8}{9}\right)^2$

3. $\frac{2^2}{3}$

4. $\left(\frac{9}{10}\right)^2$

5. $\left(\frac{2}{3}\right)^{-3}$

6. $\left(\frac{1}{2}\right)^5$

7. $\frac{3^2}{8}$

8. $\frac{3^3}{4}$

9. $\left(\frac{5}{7}\right)^{-2}$

10. If Carlos cubes a fraction and gets $\frac{27}{64}$ for an answer, what is his original fraction? Explain how you know.

11. LaTonya raised $\frac{5}{7}$ to the $^{-}2$ power and thinks $\frac{25}{49}$ is the answer. Is she correct? Explain how you know.

0-7696-4038-9 *Problem Solving*

Name ______________________ Date __________

Scientific Notation

Scientific notation is used to write very large and very small numbers. A number in scientific notation is the product of a number between 1 and 10 and a power of 10.

Examples: $4.5 \times 10^{7} = 45{,}000{,}000$ $\quad$ $6.25 \times 10^{-6} = 0.00000625$

The exponent on the power of 10 tells which way the decimal point moves.

Directions: Solve these problems. When appropriate, write your answers in scientific notation.

1. The distance between Detroit and San Francisco is about 2,500 miles. The distance around the equator is about 2.5×10^{4} miles.

a. How much further is a trip around the equator than a trip from Detroit to San Francisco?

b. How many times as long is a trip around the equator as a trip from Detroit to San Francisco?

2. Suppose you drove a car at 50 miles per hour.

a. How many hours would it take to drive from Detroit to San Francisco?

b. How many hours would it take to drive around the equator?

c. How many hours longer is a trip around the equator than a trip from Detroit to San Francisco?

d. How many times as long is a trip around the equator as a trip from Detroit to San Francisco?

EXTENDING

Use a map of the United States to find cities that are approximately 1×10^{1}, 1×10^{2}, and 1×10^{3} miles from where you live. How far are these cities from one another? Write these distances in scientific notation.

0-7696-4038-9 *Problem Solving*

Name ______________________ Date ___________

Squares and Square Roots

Directions: Respond to the following items.

1. Examine the square shown here.

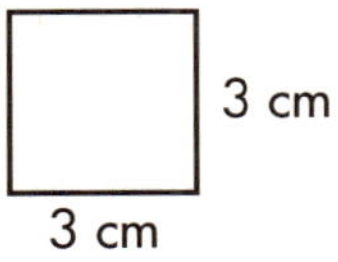

a. How does the expression 3^2 relate to the square?

b. How does the expression $\sqrt{(3^2)}$ relate to the square?

c. How do the expressions 3^2 and $\sqrt{(3^2)}$ relate to each other?

2. The side lengths of each square are given. Find the area of each square. Write number sentences to show how you found your answers.

a.

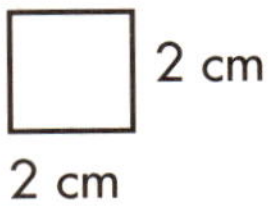

A = __________

____

b.

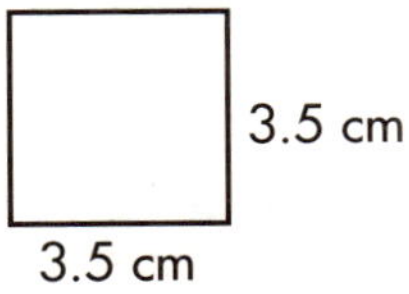

A = __________

____

c.

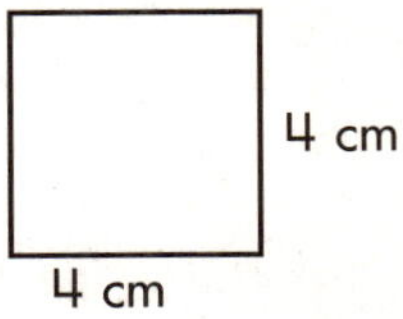

A = __________

____

0-7696-4038-9 *Problem Solving*

Name ______________________ Date __________

Squares and Square Roots (cont.)

3. The area of each square is given. Find the side lengths of each square. You may need to use a calculator. Write number sentences to show how you found your answers.

a. A = 6.25 cm^2 s

s = __________

____

b. A = 20.25 cm^2 s

s = __________

____

c. A = 25 cm^2 s

s = __________

____

4. This table shows the side lengths and areas of squares. Fill in the missing values.

Side Length (cm)	5		6.50			9	10.5			18
Area (cm^2)		30.25		49	56.25			121	240.25	

5. Explain how to find the area of a square if you know the length of one side.

6. Explain how to find the side lengths of a square if you know the area of the square.

REFLECTING

What does this activity have to do with inverse operations?

Name ______________________ Date ____________

Radicals

root to be taken (index)

$\sqrt[3]{8} = 2$

radical radicand

If the radicand is not a perfect square (perfect cube, etc.), the radical can be simplified by *extracting* perfect square (perfect cube, etc.) factors.

STEPS:	EXAMPLES: $\sqrt{72}$	$\sqrt[3]{108}$
1. Factor the radicand.	$\sqrt{2 \times 2 \times 2 \times 3 \times 3}$	$\sqrt[3]{2 \times 2 \times 3 \times 3 \times 3}$
2. Circle prime factors that occur twice for square roots (three times for cube roots, etc.).	$\sqrt{(2 \times 2) \times 2 \times (3 \times 3)}$	$\sqrt[3]{2 \times 2 \times (3 \times 3 \times 3)}$
3. Extract the roots of the circled factors. Uncircled factors stay under the radical.	$6\sqrt{2}$	$3\sqrt[3]{4}$

Directions: Use the steps to simplify the following radicals.

1. $\sqrt{45}$

____

____

____

2. $\sqrt{200}$

____

____

____

3. $\sqrt{180}$

____

____

____

4. $\sqrt[3]{40}$

____

____

____

5. $\sqrt[3]{54}$

____

____

____

6. $\sqrt[3]{375}$

____

____

____

EXPLAINING

Describe to a classmate how to extract a perfect square or a perfect cube from a radicand.

0-7696-4038-9 *Problem Solving*

Name ______________________ Date __________

Order of Operations

Mathematicians have agreed on a standard order of operations. The following phrase may help you remember the order. Each letter in the phrase stands for a mathematical operation. When simplifying equations, follow the order from top to bottom.

Please	**P**arentheses
Excuse	**E**xponents (includes roots)
My	**M**ultiplication
Dear	**D**ivision
Aunt	**A**ddition
Sally	**S**ubtraction

Directions: Vichar solved the problems below. Check each one, using the order of operations. If he solved incorrectly, explain what he did wrong.

1. $35 + 50 + \frac{25}{5} \times 5 - (8 + 11) = 431$

2. $(^-16 + 20)^2 + 6 \div (6 - 4) + \sqrt{49} = 11$

3. $\frac{1}{2}(^-12 - 8) + \sqrt{(16 + 9)} = {^-5}$

4. $15 - 8 \times 2 + 11 + 5^2 \times 2 = 100$

5. $5 - 48 \div (12 + 4) - \sqrt{\frac{4}{9}} = 1\frac{1}{3}$

6. $\sqrt[3]{64} \div (4 \times 5 - 36 \div 2) + {^-3} = {^-4}$

7. $\sqrt[3]{5(20 - 2) + \frac{30}{2} + 6 \times 3 + 2} = 25$

8. $2^3 - \sqrt[3]{^-19 + 2 + (1 + 4)^2} = 6$

0-7696-4038-9 *Problem Solving*

Name ______________________ Date ____________

Ratios

A **ratio** is basically a size comparison of two numbers based on division.

Example: There are twice as many boys in an after-school hip-hop dance program as there are girls. This relationship (ratio) may be expressed in a number of ways.

2:1 (boys : girls)	"2 to 1"	$\frac{2}{1}$

Directions: Answer each of the questions involving ratio-related situations.

1. A dessert calls for 3 cups of flour and 1 cup of sugar. It serves 4 people. If the recipe must be altered to serve 12 people, how many cups of flour will be needed for the altered recipe?

2. A theater manager notices that the ratio of people viewing comedy movies as compared to the number of people viewing action movies is 5:3. If 200 people watch comedies, how many people watch action movies?

3. A car model is listed on the box as being 1:36 scale. If a piece on the model is exactly 1 inch in length, how many feet would the actual piece be on a full-sized car?

4. A doctor has noticed there are 240 patients in a hospital with health insurance, while 60 patients are without health insurance. What is a simplified ratio to express the number of insured patients to the number without insurance?

5. If one-fifth of teenagers fail the first time they take their driver's license test, how many teenagers might reasonably be expected to fail if 15 have signed up for the test on a particular Saturday morning?

6. An artist had prints produced of his favorite painting. The original painting is 36 inches in length by 24 inches in width. He will produce 1,000 prints. If the prints are to be two-thirds the size of the original, what are the dimensions of each print?

Name ______________________ Date __________

Scale

A map is a scale drawing of a region.
The **scale** of a map is the ratio of map distance to actual distance.

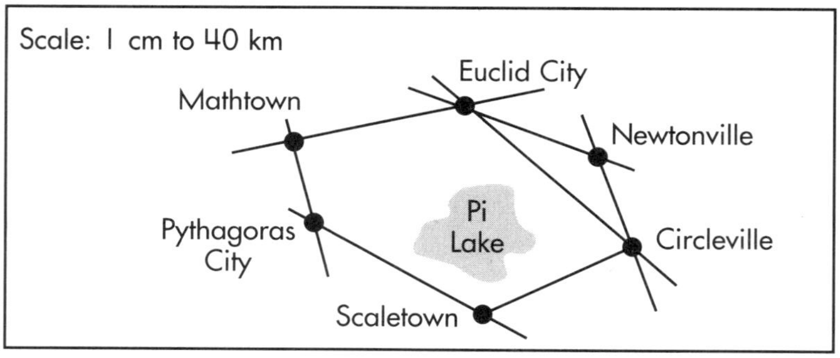

Example:
Mathtown to Pythagoras City

$$\frac{1 \text{ cm}}{40 \text{ km}} = \frac{1.1 \text{ cm}}{n}$$

$$n = 44 \text{ km}$$

Directions: Use a metric ruler to find the approximate driving distance between the following places in centimeters (cm) and kilometers (km).

1. Pythagoras City to Scaletown

2. Scaletown to Circleville

3. Circleville to Newtonville

4. Circleville to Euclid City

5. Circleville to Euclid City via Newtonville

6. Euclid City to Mathtown

7. Euclid City to Pythagoras City via Mathtown

8. Estimate the size of Pi Lake.

A drawing has a scale $\frac{1}{4}$ in.:12 ft. How long is each length on the drawing?

9. 8 ft. __________

10. 24 ft. __________

11. 30 ft. __________

12. 48 ft. __________

13. 6 ft. __________

14. 18 ft. __________

EXTENDING

Can a 15' x 25' room be drawn on an $8\frac{1}{2}$" x 11" piece of paper using a scale $\frac{1}{2}$":1'? Give a reason for your answer.

0-7696-4038-9 *Problem Solving*

Name ______________________ Date ____________

Scale Factor

Directions: A model of the new Freedom Tower being built in New York City is $\frac{1}{592}$ the size of the real skyscraper. The Freedom Tower is planned for completion in 2009.

1. The model stands 3 ft. tall. How tall will the actual building be? Why do you think this height is considered to be a symbol of American freedom?

2. The first 1.858 ft. of the model will be used as occupied space. How tall will the occupied portion of the Freedom Tower stand?

3. Above the occupied portion of the building is 400 ft. of space dedicated to windmills, which will supply 20% of the building's power. How much space on the model is dedicated to the windmills?

4. The Freedom Tower will be topped by a 276-ft. spire. How long is the spire on top of the model?

5. The model of the Freedom Tower has an antenna that brings its final height to 3.38 ft. To what height will the antenna on top of the actual building reach?

EXPLAINING

Describe the strategies you used to solve these proportion problems.

Name ______________________ Date ____________

Percentages over 100

Directions: Consider each situation to develop your knowledge of percentages.

1. Liandra buys $65 worth of clothes at her favorite store in the mall. The sales tax in her state is 8%.

a. Liandra will have to pay 100% of her purchase plus an extra 8% for sales tax. What percentage of the retail price will she have to pay altogether? __________

b. Write this percentage as a decimal. __________

c. Use this decimal value to find the total amount Liandra will have to give the salesclerk. Show your work. ____

2. The marketing department is expected to boost sales 250% in the next year. This year the company sold 450,000,000 units of products.

a. Write this percentage as a decimal. __________

b. How many times greater do the sales have to be to meet the company's goal? __________

c. How many units does the company have to sell next year to meet its goal? Show your work. ____

3. The school play was very successful. There were $3\frac{1}{4}$ times more people attending this year compared to last year. Only 80 people attended the play last year. By what percentage did the attendance change? How many people attended the play this year? Show all of your work.

EXPLAINING

Describe three more real-life situations where percentages greater than 100 may be used.

0-7696-4038-9 *Problem Solving*

Name ______________________ Date ____________

Sales Tax

A **sales tax** is a fee assessed on the value of goods or services sold. It is an example of a percentage being used for computing part of a financial transaction. The formula to calculate sales tax is: tax rate x price of item = sales tax	Example: Carla is planning to buy a large-screen television. The retail price of the television is $1,225. The tax rate where she lives is 5%. What will the sales tax be on this purchase? 0.05 x $1,225 = sales tax $61.25 = sales tax

Directions: For each of the purchases below, compute the sales tax.

1. $12,000 with 1.25% tax rate __________
2. $69.99 with 3.4% tax rate __________
3. $120.75 with 6.66% tax rate __________
4. $0.88 with 5% tax rate __________
5. $55,000 with 7.5% tax rate __________
6. $8.50 with 9% tax rate __________
7. Jorge is buying a new computer. A system he likes is priced at $1,099. If the sales tax is 4.25%, how much sales tax would he owe on this purchase?
8. Marcine is buying business equipment, which will cost $2,700. If the sales tax is 5%, what will be her total cost for the equipment?
9. The local newsstand must collect a sales tax of 2% on printed materials and a sales tax of 4% on all other goods. What total sales tax will a customer owe if buying a magazine for $4.95 and a box of candy for $0.80?
10. Sarah was charged $1.80 sales tax on a purchase of $16.40. If the sales tax rate is 4.5%, how much was she overcharged in sales tax?

REFLECTING

What are the financial implications for a state with a high sales tax rate that borders a state with no sales tax?

0-7696-4038-9 *Problem Solving*

Name ______________________ Date ___________

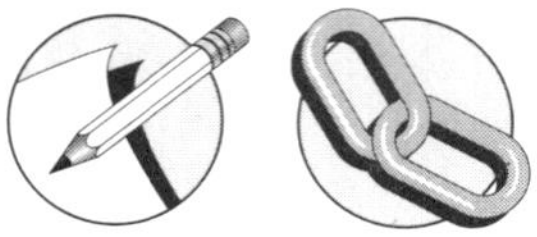

Commission

A **commission** is a percentage-based compensation, ordinarily paid to a person who is involved in the sale of some product. Typically sales personnel will earn a commission for items they are able to sell for a business.

The formula to calculate commission is:
commission rate x price of item = commission earned

Directions: Compute the commission for each of the situations below.

1. Joaquin is given a $\frac{1}{4}$% commission for advising a client on the closing of a deal worth \$1,200,000. How much does Joaquin earn?

2. Martin is paid a commission rate of 11.75% for the sale of livestock and a commission rate of 3.5% for hay and grain sold. How much money will Martin earn in commissions during a month in which he sells \$15,600 in livestock and \$20,340 in hay and grain?

3. Shonda is considering a sales job. She currently earns a fixed salary of \$18,200 per year. The sales job she is considering offers no fixed salary but an 8% commission rate on sales made by employees. Shonda was told that the top salesperson at this company closed \$320,000 in sales the previous year. How much more did the top salesperson earn than Shonda?

4. Mallorie took a 15-minute break from her sales job at a computer store. The cash register clerk who filled in for her sold a \$2,610 computer system, thus earning the commission for that sale. How much money did Mallorie lose while on break if her commission rate was 1.75%, considering the computer sale would ordinarily have been hers?

EXPLAINING

Instead of paying employees commissions on sales, why would some businesses rather pay employees a salary based on how well they work with customers or on how well the business is doing overall? Discuss your thoughts with a classmate.

Name ______________________ Date ____________

Interest

Interest is a charge for borrowed money, generally a percentage of the amount borrowed. You can also earn interest on invested money (like in a savings account).

To calculate interest:
interest = principal amount x rate x time

Directions: Calculate the interest for each of the situations below. Show your work so you can explain and justify your answers.

1. Jay bought a certificate of deposit at a bank for $10,000. He agreed to leave his money with the bank for one year at an interest rate of $7\frac{1}{2}$%. How much money will Jay earn in interest on his deposit of $10,000?

2. Lucinda is considering buying a new computer that costs $880.00. She has the money in her savings account, which is currently earning 5.5% interest per year. If she waits one year before buying the new computer, how much interest will she be able to collect on her money?

3. Rita took out a $2,000 loan. The loan was made through a finance company at an interest rate of 23.99% per year. How much interest will Rita owe if the loan is not repaid before the year ends?

4. Luc owns a local business. He arranges a one-month loan with his bank in order to stock extra inventory for a special sale he is advertising. Luc borrowed $20,000 at $1\frac{1}{2}$% interest for this one-month period. How much money will Luc need to repay the bank at the end of the month?

5. Angie has $12,200 in a savings account that pays 8% interest per year. She knows she will need $13,000 in exactly one year to meet her daughter's tuition payment. Will there be enough money in her account in a year's time to meet this obligation?

Name ____________________ Date __________

Financial Math in Context

Directions: Solve the problems below. Explain how you found each answer.

1. Emil is going to use money from his savings account to buy a new car. He has $26,400 in his account. Where Emil lives, sales tax on this kind of purchase is $4\frac{1}{4}$%. If the car he is planning to buy costs $24,244.33 before the sales tax is added, how much money will Emil have left in his account after buying the car and paying the sales tax?

2. Last year Stewart was paid a base salary of $12,000 per year and a commission of 3% on the total dollar value of sales he closed. He sold $1,120,000 worth of company products. This year his boss announced that Stewart's new commission rate would be cut to 2.8% on sales, but his base salary will be raised to $14,000 per year. This has given Stewart cause for concern. How much less money would Stewart have made last year if this plan had been in place then?

3. A painting by a famous Impressionist sold through an auction house by private treaty, meaning that the sales price was not publicly disclosed. This particular auction house works on a commission rate of 10%. If it is discovered that the commission on this painting was $400,000 what was the sale price of the painting?

4. Your Great-Uncle Eddie just passed away. Since he loved puzzles, he left you a puzzle in his will. It states that you may receive from his estate your choice of one of the following options.

Option 1: One-sixth of the selling price of an antique car he lovingly restored. Great-Uncle Eddie bought it for $500.00, but over its lifetime, it increased in value by 900%.

Option 2: One-fourth of the stock Eddie owned in PQ Cola. He bought the stock for $3,000.00, and it decreased in value by 5%.

Option 3: Three-eighths of the stock he owned in Gadget World. He bought the stock for $1,000.00, and it increased in value by 250% while he owned it.

Which option would you choose? Give a reason for your answer.

0-7696-4038-9 *Problem Solving*

Name ____________________ Date ____________

Check Your Skills—Number and Operations

1. Use the variables *a*, *b*, and *c* to explain and demonstrate three mathematical properties.

2. Simplify the following expressions.

a. $(^-8)^2 =$ __________

b. $(^-16 + 20)^2 + 6 \div (6 - 4) =$ __________

c. $7.49 \times 10^{-6} =$ __________

3. Explain how $(^-2)^3$ and $(2)^{-3}$ are related.

4. A scale drawing shows the plans for a horse barn in a 1:48 ratio. If a wall of the horse barn on the plan is 2 foot in length, how many actual feet will that wall of the horse barn be?

5. Sydney wants to take out a one-year used-car loan for $2,000. Bank One offers an interest rate of 13.99% per year, with no deposit needed. Bank Two offers an interest rate of 15% on one-year used-car loans but requires a $500 down payment. Compare these two offers and explain to Sydney which one is the better deal.

6. The marketing department in a tennis shoe company is expecting to boost sales 175% in the next year. This year the company sold 230,000,000 pairs of tennis shoes. How many pairs of shoes does the company have to sell next year to meet its goal?

Name ______________________ Date __________

Solution Methods

Directions: For each problem, try the solution method suggested. Check your work using a different strategy. Compare the results.

1. Joel's grandmother gave him $100.00 on his twelfth birthday. She told him that as long as he made the honor roll each grading period while in school, she would double that "investment" every two years. Since Joel plans on being a veterinarian, he figures he will be in school for at least ten more years. How much will his "investment" be at the end of ten years? Solution method: Make a chart.

2. The Student Council arranged chairs on the gymnasium floor for a special program. Rachel sat in a chair in a row with 7 chairs on each side of her. The row she sat in was fifth from the front and sixth from the rear. How many people can be seated in the gymnasium in all? Solution method: Draw a picture.

3. Esmé is doing a survey to see how many people have sisters and how many have brothers. Out of the 26 people she has surveyed, 18 have sisters, 14 have brothers, and 6 have both brothers and sisters. How many people have only sisters, and how many have only brothers? Solution method: Use a Venn diagram to solve this problem.

0-7696-4038-9 *Problem Solving*

Name ____________________ Date __________

Solution Methods (cont.)

4. Jamie and Josh are growing roses for their science project. This morning they found the plants covered with aphids (tiny insects that eat roses). To combat the aphids, Josh and Jamie decided to buy some ladybugs, which are natural predators of aphids. The two students count 143 aphids on one of their 14 plants. If each plant has the same number of aphids and if the ladybugs are sold in boxes of 12, how many boxes will they need to buy to have at least 1 ladybug for every 8 aphids? Solution method: Break the problem into smaller pieces.

5. An environmental habitat contains eagles and cougars. There are 40 animals, and these animals have a total of 128 feet. How many animals of each kind does the environmental habitat have? Solution method: Guess and check. Use a chart to keep track of your guesses.

6. Chandani is stocking the Snack Shack with sports beverages. She puts out twice as many bottles of tropical punch as lemon-lime, 10 more bottles of lemon-lime than fruit punch, 4 times as many bottles of fruit punch as orange, 2 fewer bottles of orange than grape, and 9 bottles of grape. How many bottles of sports beverage does Chandani put in the Snack Shack? Solution method: Work backwards.

REFLECTING

Which solution methods do you tend to favor when solving problems?

0-7696-4038-9 *Problem Solving*

Name ______________________ Date __________

Critical Thinking

Directions: Choose a solution method to solve each problem. Explain how you found your answer.

1. The highlight of the annual North Hampton Middle School game day is the championship 100-yard sack race. The sixth-grade champion gets an 80-yard head start because his fastest speed is 1 yard per second; the seventh-grade champ, who moves at 3 yards per second, gets a head start of 40 yards; and the eighth-grade champ, who moves at 5 yards per second, gets no head start. Make a chart and graph to show the racer's positions at 5 seconds and at 13 seconds. Who will win the race?

2. The Gonzalez brothers are driving cross-country. To reduce wear and tear on themselves and their car, they've decided on an unusual plan. They'll drive 250 miles the first day. On day two, they'll drive twice that far; on day three, they'll travel one-half as far as day two. On day four, they'll drive three times as far as day three; on day five, one-third as far as day four; on day six, four times as far as day five; on day seven, one-fourth as far as day six; and so on. If their cross-country trip is roughly 6,250 miles, how many days will it take them to reach their destination?

3. Natalie scored 32 points in last night's basketball game. However, her coach lost the score book, and the reporter from the local newspaper wants to know how many of each kind of goal (3-point shots, 2-point shots, and 1-point free throws) she made.

   a. What if she knows she scored three 3-pointers?

   b. What about two 2-pointers and three free throws?

   Explain your answer with numbers and words.

0-7696-4038-9 *Problem Solving*

Name ______________________ Date ____________

Critical Thinking (cont.)

4. How many stripes are on each of the four zebras at the zoo? Use the clues and chart to help you find the number of stripes on each zebra. The total number of stripes is over 200.

Clues:

- Zany has more stripes than Zelda but fewer than Zed.
- One zebra has 57 stripes.
- The difference between the highest and lowest number of stripes is 50.
- Zach has the fewest number of stripes.
- No zebra has more than 100 stripes.
- Zelda has 20 more stripes than Zach and 13 fewer than the zebra with the number of stripes closest to her own number.

Zebra's Name	Number of Stripes

5. Two large boxes of guinea pigs arrived at Ramona's pet store, Rodents 4-U, but the guinea pigs chewed their way out of the boxes before Ramona had a chance to take inventory. Ramona captured 92 guinea pigs, but she's not certain she found all of them because the guinea pigs also chewed up the packing slips. The only bits of paper she could read said that there were 19 more guinea pigs in one box than the other and that there were 3 guinea pigs in one box for every 2 in the other box. Has Ramona found all of the guinea pigs? If not, how many more does she need to find?

EXPLAINING

Describe how knowing different solution methods can help you solve complicated math problems. Discuss your answer with a classmate.

0-7696-4038-9 *Problem Solving*

Name ______________________ Date __________

Patterns

Directions: Find the missing numbers in each series. Describe the pattern algebraically.

1. 3, 8, 15, 20, _____ , 32, 39, _____ , 51, 56

Pattern ____

2. 100, 120, 140, 160, 180, _____ , _____ , _____

Pattern ____

3. 212, _____ , 134, 67, 95, 47.5

Pattern ____

4. 3, 9, 81, _____

Pattern ____

5. 1, 5, 25, 125, _____ , _____

Pattern ____

Solve for each missing part of the pattern. Then write a short description of each pattern.

6. $^{-}6$, $^{-}5$, $^{-}3$, 0, 4, _____ , _____ , _____

7. X, U, R, _____ , _____ , I, F, C

8. △△□□_____△□_____△△□□

0-7696-4038-9 *Problem Solving*

Name ______________________ Date ___________

More Patterns

Directions: Perhaps the most famous pattern ever defined is that of Leonardo of Pisa, who is also known as Fibonacci. This mathematician's work became famous in the early 1200s. After observing the proliferation of rabbits, Fibonacci defined a pattern that has implications for much of the natural world. The pattern begins 1, 1, 2, 3, 5...

1. Beginning at the 2, each following number in the series is the sum of the two previous numbers. Try filling in the values for the blanks below.

1, 1, 2, 3, 5, _____, _____, _____, _____, _____, 89, 144, _____, _____

You can see that Fibonacci's pattern is based on addition and that its members tend to rise gradually in size.

2. What if the series began with 3, 4 and maintained a pattern in which each of the two preceding members are added to form the next member? Try filling in the blanks for this variation of the Fibonacci sequence.

3, 4, _____, _____, _____, _____, 47, 76, _____, _____

Mathematicians have made observations about the ratios of numbers in the Fibonacci sequence and in the similarity of ratios in other series that employ the Fibonacci pattern. Look at the values 89 and 144 given in the Fibonacci sequence above.

$\frac{89}{144}$ = 0.618055 (carried only to 6 decimal places)

Now look at the second series.

$\frac{47}{76}$ = 0.618421 (carried only to 6 decimal places)

3. Work with a partner to create your own variation of the Fibonacci sequence. Carry out your series to about 20 members. Try comparing the ratios of its members to those of the Fibonacci sequence. What observation can you make about the ratios you've found compared to those of the original Fibonacci sequence?

0-7696-4038-9 *Problem Solving*

Name ______________________ Date ____________

Expressions

Directions: Study each math expression. Find the matching expression and write that letter on the line next to each problem.

_______ **1.** sum of x and y

_______ **2.** x squared decreased by y

_______ **3.** difference of x and y

_______ **4.** x less than y

_______ **5.** triple x minus y

_______ **6.** twice x increased by y

_______ **7.** product of x and y

_______ **8.** quotient of x and y

_______ **9.** x more than double y

_______ **10.** cube of x diminished by y

A. $x - y$ **C.** $2y + x$ **E.** $y - x$ **G.** $2x + y$ **I.** $x + y$

B. $x^2 - y$ **D.** $3x - y$ **F.** $x^3 - y$ **H.** $\frac{x}{y}$ **J.** xy

Match each sentence to an equivalent math statement.

_______ **11.** Twice x is 4 more than y.

_______ **12.** X less than y is 4.

_______ **13.** Y more than x is less than 4.

_______ **14.** Four less than x is less than y.

_______ **15.** Y less than x is less than 4.

_______ **16.** X is less than twice y.

_______ **17.** Twice x plus 4 is y.

_______ **18.** Four less than x is y.

_______ **19.** Y more than twice x is 4.

_______ **20.** Twice x is more than $4y$.

K. $2x + y = 4$ **M.** $y - x = 4$ **O.** $x < 2y$ **Q.** $x - 4 = y$ **S.** $x - y < 4$

L. $x + y < 4$ **N.** $x - 4 < y$ **P.** $2x = 4 + y$ **R.** $2x + 4 = y$ **T.** $2x > 4y$

EXTENDING

Write several expressions in both numerical and word form. Exchange them with a classmate and see if he or she can write matching answers.

Name ______________________ Date ____________

Writing and Solving Equations

Directions: Write an equation to model each situation, using the variables given. Then make a table of data pairs that fit the situation. Use graph paper to make a graph to display the data in the table. Finally, solve the problem.

1. Jamel's landlord gave him \$50 for agreeing to keep the walkway cleared all winter. Jamal will also earn \$8 each day he has to shovel snow. How many days did he shovel snow if he earned \$170 for the season?

A = amount earned D = # of days worked

2. Emma rode her bike 15 miles in the morning. In the afternoon, she averaged a speed of 10 miles per hour. If she rode a total of 47.5 miles that day, how long did she spend on her bike that afternoon?

D = distance traveled H = hours biked

3. Javier has already scored 4 soccer goals this season. If he can score 3 goals per game for the rest of the season, how long will it take him to reach a total of 30 goals?

T = total number of goals G = number of games played

0-7696-4038-9 *Problem Solving*

Name ______________________ Date __________

Writing and Solving Equations (cont.)

4. Tanequa's motor scooter gets 45 miles per gallon. She fills the tank and then travels 360 miles before running out of gas. How much gas does the tank hold?

M = number of miles traveled N = number of gallons the tank holds

5. Caleb has already typed 100 words of his paper. If he can average 60 words a minute from this point on, how long will it take him to type a 725-word paper?

W = number of words typed T = time

6. Malik works in a youth day camp during the summer. Each day he must bring 3 pieces of fruit per child. On this day Malik brings 135 pieces of fruit. How many children were at camp this day?

F = total pieces of fruit C = number of children

REFLECTING

What do all of these problem situations have in common? Compare their equations, graphs, and tables.

Name ______________________ Date ___________

Equations in Context

Directions: Solve the problems below. Show all of your work.

1. Estelle wants to buy a set of dishes at an auction. She will owe a 5% buyer's commission as well as a 6.5% sales tax on the price of the dishes.

a. Write an equation expressing the total cost, C, of her purchase if she bids p dollars on the dishes.

b. If she has $300, what is the largest amount she can bid on the dishes?

2. One car rental agency charges a flat fee of $50 plus $0.25 per mile. Another charges a flat fee of $40 plus $0.40 per mile.

a. For each agency, write an equation expressing the cost, C, of traveling m miles.

Agency 1: $C =$

Agency 2: $C =$

b. If you plan on traveling 115 miles total, which is the better deal? What if you plan on traveling only 65 miles?

c. Use agency ____ if you plan on traveling less than ____ miles. Use agency ____ if you plan on traveling more than ____ miles.

3. Akim wants to sell his coin collection. Golden Hammer Auction House charges a 15% commission. Heavy Gavel Auction House charges a listing fee of $500 and only a 12% commission.

a. For each auction house, write an equation expressing the commission price, C, if the collection sells for p dollars.

Golden Hammer: $C =$

Heavy Gavel: $C =$

b. If the coins sell for $25,000, which firm should Akim use?

0-7696-4038-9 *Problem Solving*

Name ______________________ Date __________

One- and Two-Step Equations

Directions: Solve the following one-step equations. Put your answers back into the original equations to prove your answers are correct.

1. $^{-}20 + x = 11$

2. $^{-}16 = 23 - x$

3. $^{-}7 = {}^{-}10 + x$

4. $53 - x = 72$

5. $x - 27 = {}^{-}4$

6. $12 = 6 - x$

Find the solutions to these two-step equations. Use inverse operations to prove your answers are correct.

7. $\frac{y}{5} + 11 = 18$

8. $5r - 140 = {}^{-}15$

9. $\frac{n}{^{-}7} - 5 = 4$

10. $38 - \frac{a}{11} = 34$

11. $86 = {}^{-}5m + 11$

12. $9 = 21 - \frac{c}{9}$

Simplify the following expressions. Then solve for the variables.

13. $4(f - 3) + 3(f + 2) = 50$

14. $(5w + 7) - (2w + 5) = 53$

EXTENDING

When Juanita is as old as her mother is now, she will be five times as old as her son is now. By then Juanita's son will be eight years older then Juanita is now. Juanita's age, combined with her mother's age, equals 100 years. How old is Juanita's son? Write an equation and solve for the variable.

Name ____________________ Date ____________

Solving Equations: Scrambled Steps

Directions: For each problem, help Geoffrey unscramble the steps. Rewrite the steps in the correct order to solve each linear equation. Check your answer in the original equation to prove it is correct.

1. $2(x - 3) + 4x = 8 - x$

A. $7x - 6 = 8$
B. $2x - 6 + 4x = 8 - x$
C. $7x = 14$
D. $6x - 6 = 8 - x$
E. $x = 2$

$2(x - 3) + 4x = 8 - x$
____
____
____
____
____

2. $5 - 3(x - 2) = 4(x + 1)$

A. $7 = 7x$
B. $11 - 3x = 4x + 4$
C. $1 = x$
D. $11 = 7x + 4$
E. $5 - 3x + 6 = 4x + 4$

$5 - 3(x - 2) = 4(x + 1)$
____
____
____
____
____

3. $^{-}6x - 2(x + 1) = x + 7$

A. $^{-}2 = 9x + 7$
B. $^{-}1 = x$
C. $^{-}8x - 2 = x + 7$
D. $^{-}6x - 2x - 2 = x + 7$
E. $^{-}9 = 9x$

$^{-}6x - 2(x + 1) = x + 7$
____
____
____
____
____

4. $3(2x - 1) = 7 + 2(x - 5)$

A. $6x - 3 = 2x - 3$
B. $6x - 3 = 7 + 2x - 10$
C. $4x = 0$
D. $x = 0$
E. $4x - 3 = {}^{-}3$

$3(2x - 1) = 7 + 2(x - 5)$
____
____
____
____
____

EXTENDING

Write your own linear equation and solve for the variable. Share your equation with a classmate.

0-7696-4038-9 *Problem Solving*

Name ______________________ Date __________

Functions

A simple algebraic **function** exists between two variables when there is a corresponding relationship between one variable and the value of the other.

Example: Is y a function of x in the following expression?

$$y = 4x$$

If values are inserted for x, it is easy to determine a corresponding value for y. For example, if 1 is inserted for the value of x, then y becomes 4.

$$y = 4(1)$$
$$y = 4$$

Another way to write this same function is in terms of only one variable.

$$f(x) = 4x$$

This way of writing a function uses $f(x)$ as a substitute for y. It means essentially the same thing. When a value for x is inserted in the expression, a corresponding $f(x)$ value is created.

Directions: For each of the functions, find the value of that function using the information given.

1. $y = 2x + 1$

a. $y =$ ______ when x is 4.

b. $y =$ ______ when x is 7.

2. $y = x - 1$

a. $y =$ ______ when x is 0.

b. $y =$ ______ when x is 3.

3. $f(x) = \frac{x}{2}$

a. $f(x) =$ ______ when x is 4.

b. $f(x) =$ ______ when x is 1.

4. $f(p) = 3p$

a. $f(p) =$ ______ when p is $\frac{1}{2}$.

b. $f(p) =$ ______ when p is $^-2$.

5. $y = (x)^2$

a. $y =$ ______ when x is 2.

b. $y =$ ______ when x is $^-4$.

6. $f(m) = \sqrt[3]{m}$

a. $f(m) =$ __________ when m is 8.

b. $f(m) =$ __________ when m is $\frac{27}{64}$.

0-7696-4038-9 *Problem Solving*

Name ____________________ Date ____________

Linear and Nonlinear Functions

Directions: Use your knowledge of linear and nonlinear graphs to answer the following questions.

1. Describe how to tell whether a function is linear by looking at its graph.

2. Look at each of the following graphs and equations. Identify each function as either linear or nonlinear. Justify your answers.

a. $y = x^2 - 6x + 10$

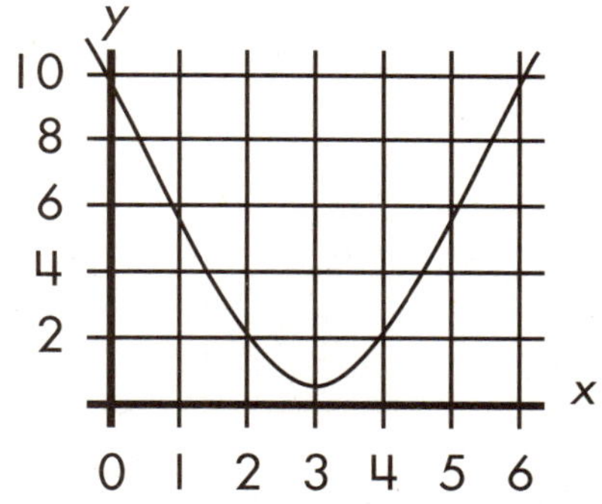

____

c. $y = 2x + 1$

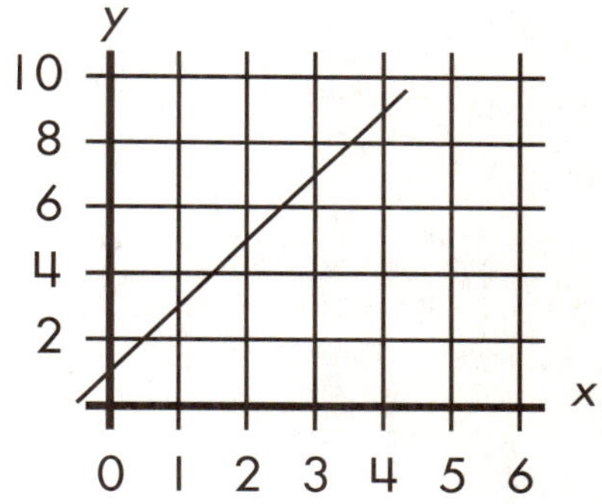

____

b. $y = 10 - \frac{5}{3}x$

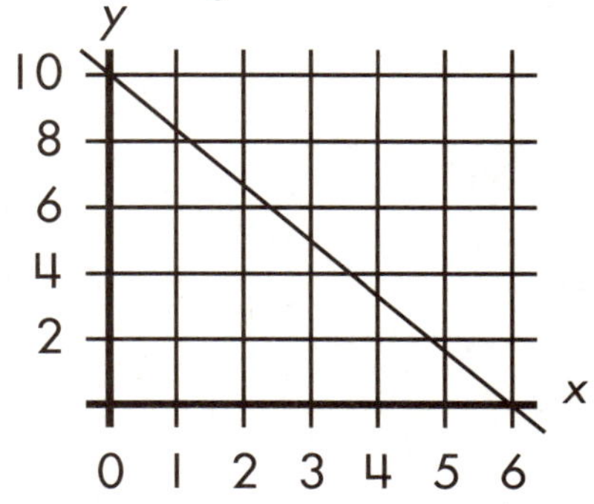

____

d. $y = 2^x$

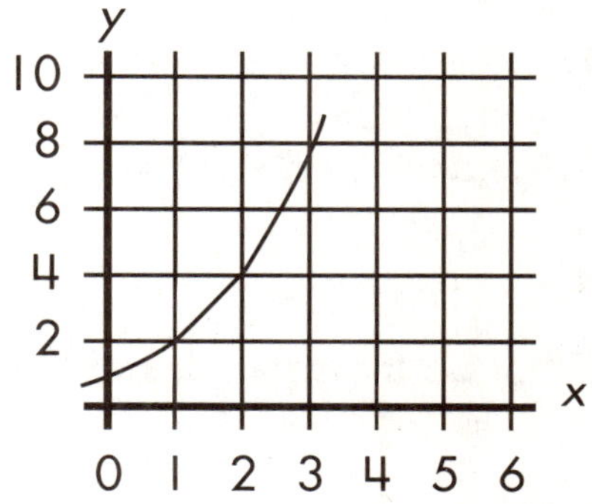

____

0-7696-4038-9 *Problem Solving*

Name ______________________ Date ____________

Linear and Nonlinear Functions (cont.)

e. $y = 10(0.75)^x$

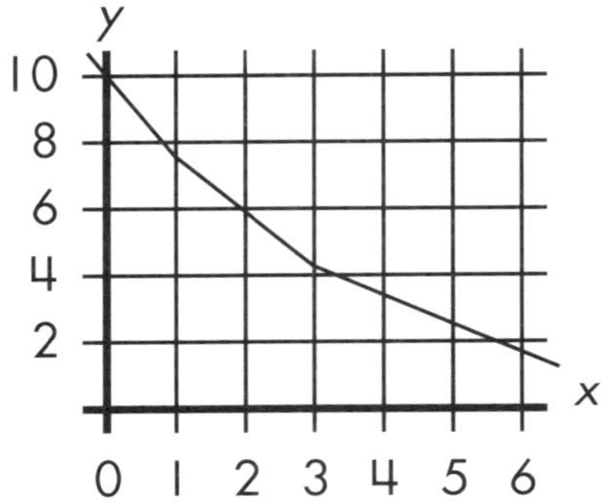

____

g. $y = \frac{1}{2}x$

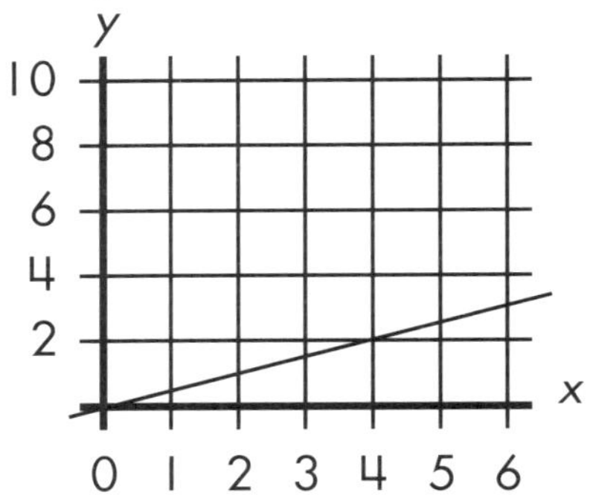

____

f. $y = {}^{-}x^2 + 6x + 1$

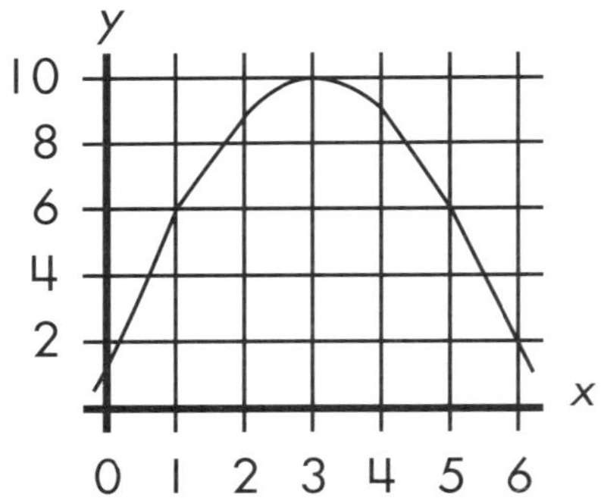

____

h. $y = 10 - x$

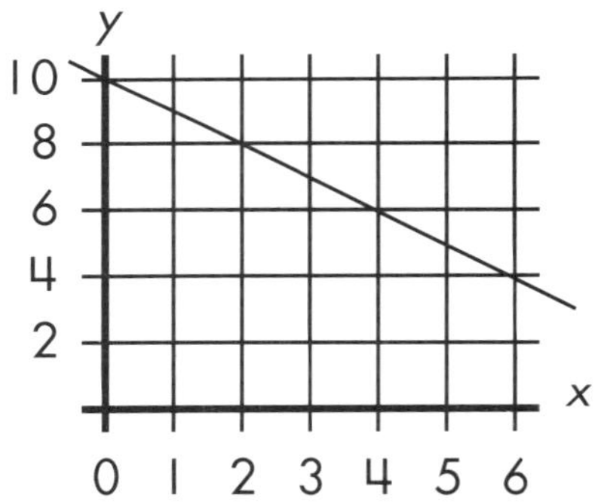

____

3. What do the equations of the linear functions have in common?

4. What do the equations of the nonlinear functions have in common?

EXTENDING

Make a table of data pairs for each graph. What do the tables of linear functions have in common? What do the tables of nonlinear functions have in common?

Name ______________________ Date ___________

Graphs and Relationships

Directions: Which graph most likely shows the following? Write the letter on the line.

A. relationship between centimeters and inches
B. pairs of possible positive integer factors of 24
C. cost of postage compared to weight
D. resale value of a car based on its age
E. growth of virus over time
F. time awake versus time asleep

1. _____

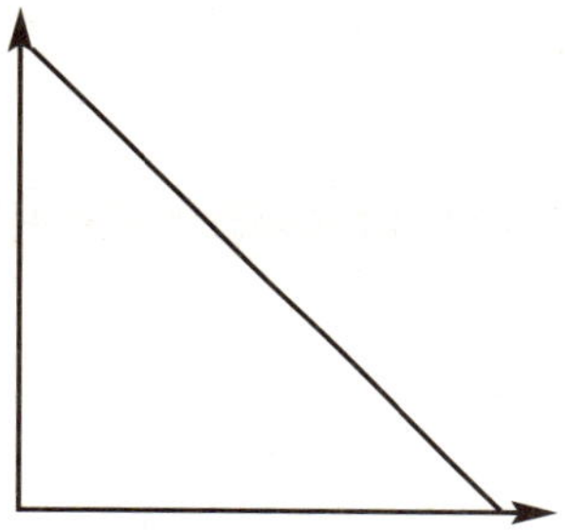

2. _____

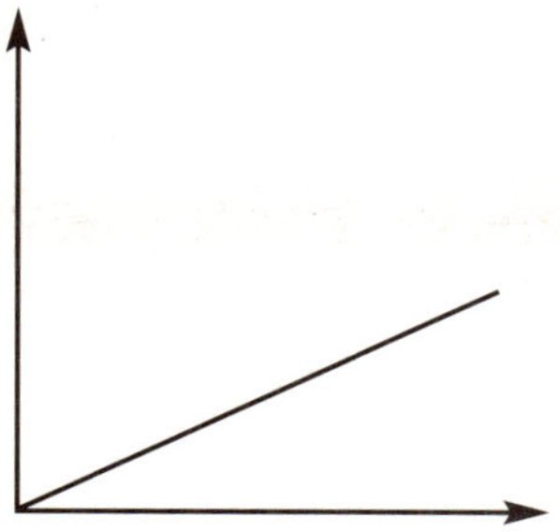

3. _____

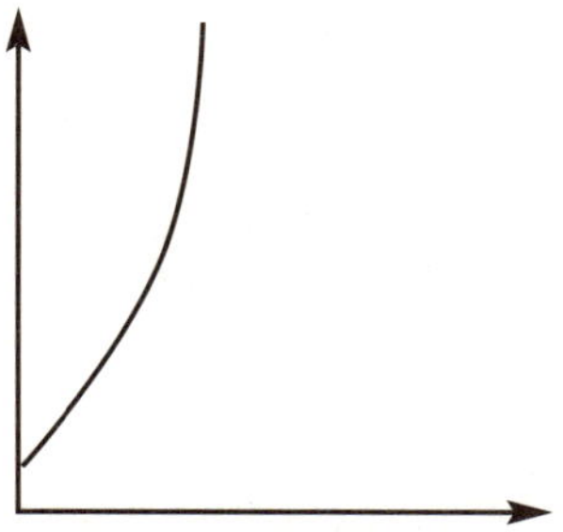

4. _____

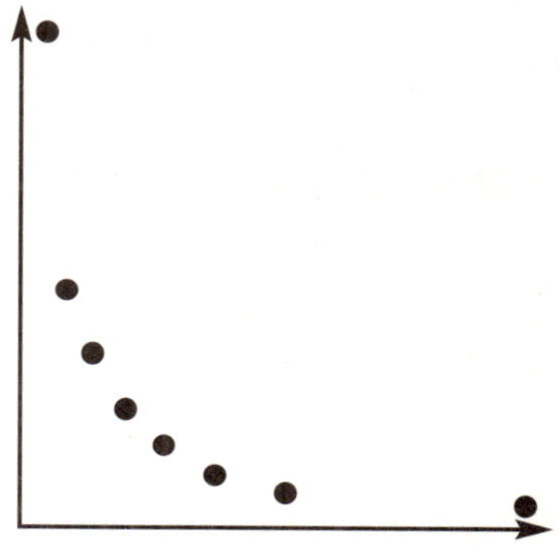

5. _____

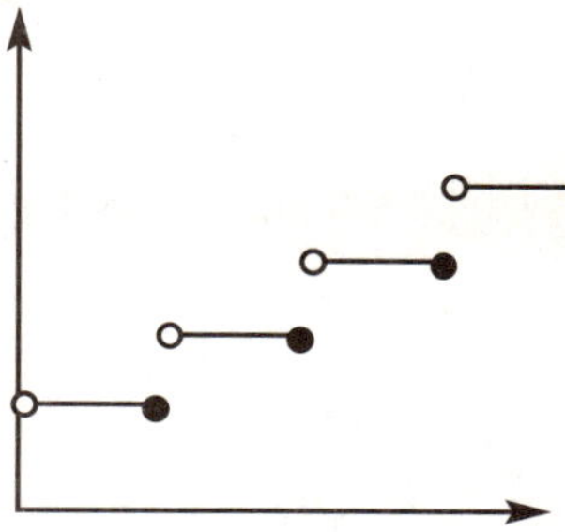

6. _____

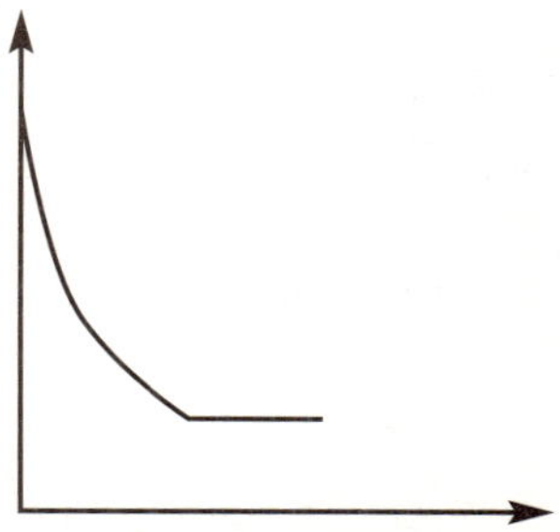

0-7696-4038-9 *Problem Solving*

Name ______________________ Date __________

Coordinate Plane Graphing

A **coordinate plane** provides grid work for specifying locations in a visual format. Those locations are specified by an (*x*, *y*) coordinate pair.

Look at the simple equation $y = 2x$. By taking several *x* values (such as $x = 1, 2, 3, 4$) and plugging those values into the equation one at a time, corresponding *y* values can be determined, thereby providing a coordinate pair. For example, when *x* is 1, the value of *y* is 2. When *x* is 2, the value of *y* is 4. When *x* is 3, the value of *y* is 6. And when *x* is 4, the value of *y* is 8. Coordinate pairs for each of those groups of points can then be made: (1, 2) (2, 4) (3, 6) (4, 8). Those points can be plotted on an appropriate graph.

Directions: Use the graph below to answer the questions. Depending on the information given, provide either a point or a coordinate pair.

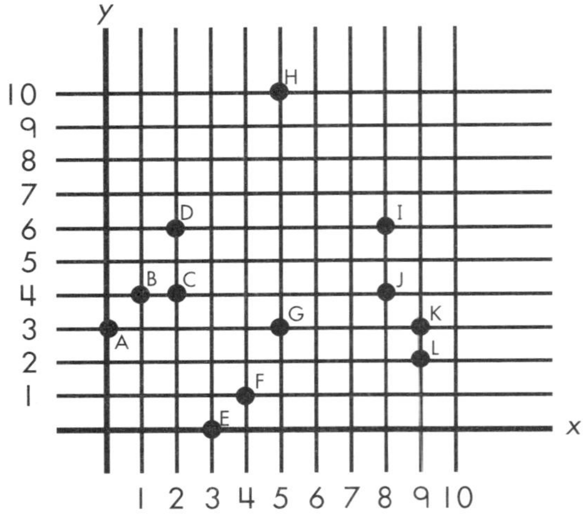

1. G(,)

2. K(,)

3. B(,)

4. A(,)

5. (9, 2) _____

6. (2, 4) _____

7. (4, 1) _____

8. (8, 4) _____

0-7696-4038-9 *Problem Solving*

Name ______________________ Date ___________

Coordinate Plane Graphing (cont.)

Use the graph on page 48 to answer the following questions.

9. What is the area of the rectangle formed by points D, C, J, I? _______

10. What coordinate pair would form a rectangle when associated with points G, K, L? _______

11. Which two points have the most distance between them compared to all of the other points indicated on this graph? _______

12. Name the points that are found at $y = 4$ on this graph. _______

13. Do the points on this graph appear to represent an equation, such as $y = 2x$? Why or why not?

14. Suppose this graph actually represents a salesperson's territory. The *x*-axis indicates Elm Street; the *y*-axis, Oak Street. If the points represent households who have previously bought merchandise, can any conclusions be drawn from the information presented?

15. What conclusion might you, as a detective, draw if the graph represented robberies of convenience stores in a neighborhood and you were studying the graph? Would the information become more relevant if only the convenience store at coordinates (6, 2) had not been robbed?

0-7696-4038-9 *Problem Solving*

Name ______________________ Date __________

The Equation of a Line

Slope is the ratio of $\frac{\text{rise}}{\text{run}}$ and indicates the steepness of the graph of a line.
The **rise** is the vertical change, and the **run** is the horizontal change.
Slope can be determined from the coordinates of two points on a line.

Examples: (2, 3) and (4, 9)

$\frac{\text{rise}}{\text{run}} = \frac{9 - 3}{4 - 2}$ = positive slope of $\frac{6}{2}$ or 3

(6, 1) and (${}^{-}2$, 4)

$\frac{\text{rise}}{\text{run}} = \frac{4 - 1}{{}^{-}2 - 6}$ = negative slope of $\frac{{}^{-}3}{8}$

Directions: Examine each of the graphs and answer the corresponding questions.

1. Here are the equations of 4 different lines. Make a table of (x, y) coordinate pairs for each equation. Find at least 3 points on each line. Then graph all 4 lines on the same grid.

A. $y = x$

B. $y = 2 + x$

C. $y = {}^{-}5 + x$

D. $y = {}^{-}3 + x$

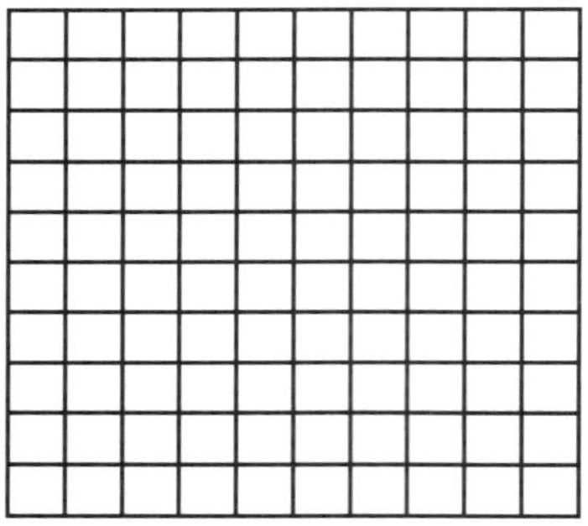

2. What is the same about all of the graphs? ______________________

3. What is different about all of the graphs? ______________________

4. What is the same about all of the equations? ______________________

5. What is different about all of the equations? ______________________

0-7696-4038-9 *Problem Solving*

Name ______________________ Date ____________

The Equation of a Line (cont.)

6. Here are the equations of 4 different lines. Make a table of (x, y) coordinate pairs for each equation. Find at least 3 points on each line. Then graph all 4 lines on the same grid.

A. $y = 5 + \frac{1}{2}x$ **B.** $y = 5 + 2x$ **C.** $y = 5 + \frac{^-2}{3}x$ **D.** $y = 5 + {^-3}x$

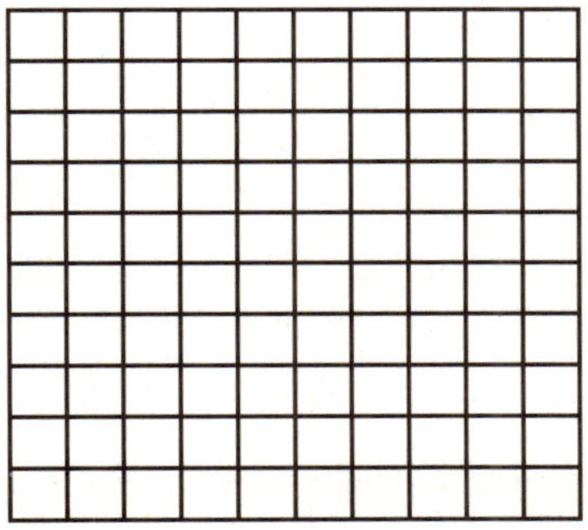

7. What is the same about all of the graphs? ______________________________

8. What is different about all of the graphs? ______________________________

9. What is the same about all of the equations? ______________________________

10. What is different about all of the equations? ______________________________

EXPLAINING

Explain how to analyze the equation of a line to tell how the graph will look.

0-7696-4038-9 *Problem Solving*

Name ______________________ Date __________

Linear Equations: Finding Intercepts

When an equation is in **a**x + **b**y = **c** form,
use the x-intercept and the y-intercept to graph the line.

Graph $3x - 4y = 12$.

To find the x-intercept, let $y = 0$.
$3x - 4(0) = 12 \rightarrow x = 4 \rightarrow (4, 0)$

To find the y-intercept, let $x = 0$.
$3(0) - 4y = 12 \rightarrow y = ^{-}3 \rightarrow (0, ^{-}3)$

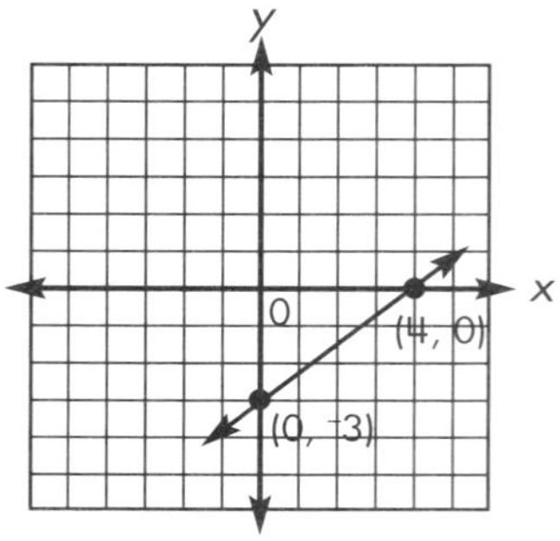

Directions: For each equation, find the intercepts, plot the points, and draw the line.

1. $2x + 3y = 6$

x	y

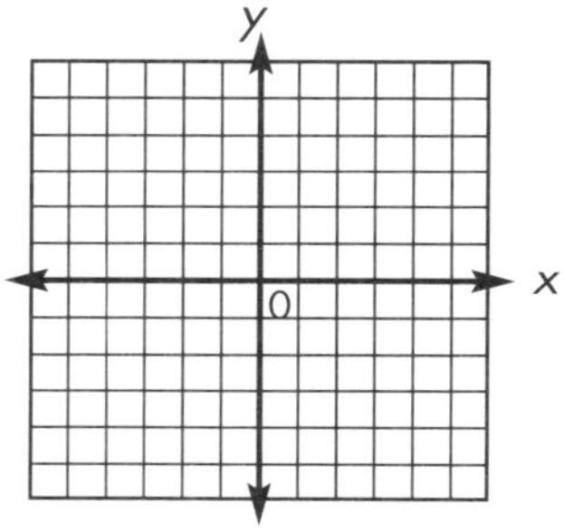

2. $x - 5y = 5$

x	y

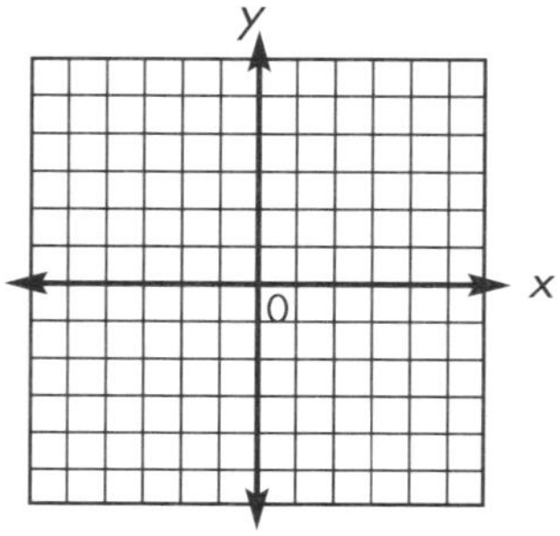

3. $2x + \frac{1}{2}y = ^{-}2$

x	y

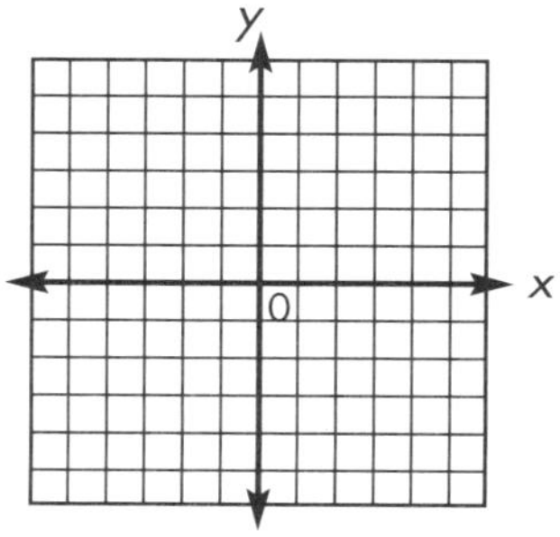

4. $2x - 5y = ^{-}10$

x	y

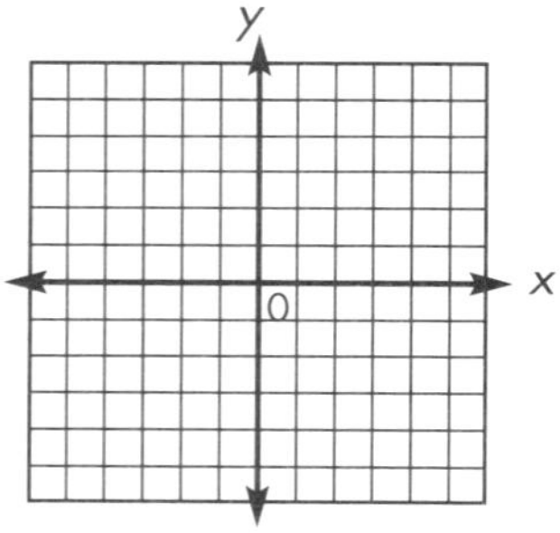

5. $x - y = ^{-}3$

x	y

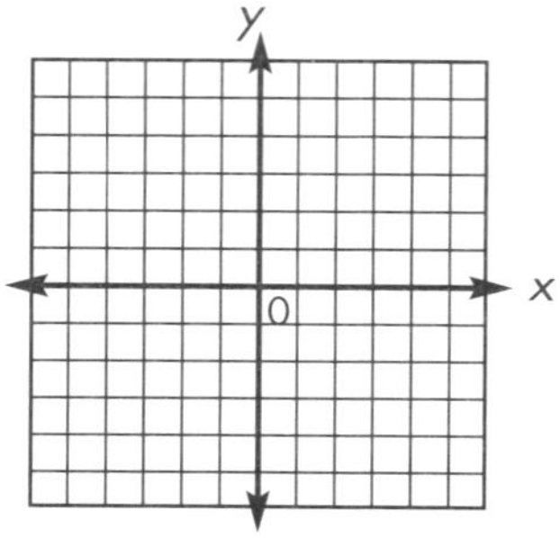

6. $x + \frac{1}{3}y = 1$

x	y

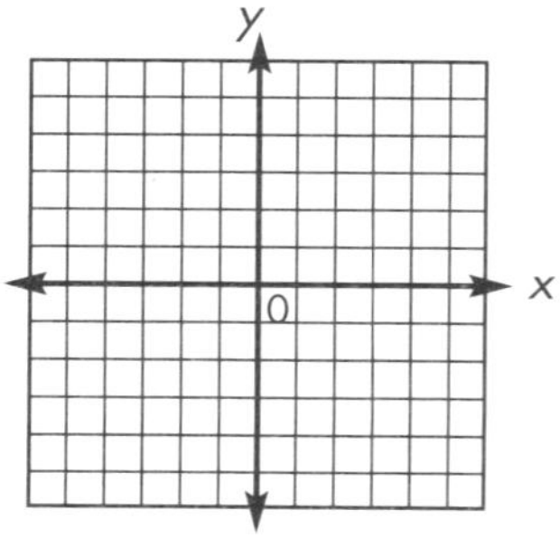

0-7696-4038-9 *Problem Solving*

Name ______________________ Date ____________

Linear Equations: Slope-Intercept Form

The slope and y-intercept can be used to draw the graph of an equation.

1. Write the equation in $y = \mathbf{m}x + \mathbf{b}$ form; **m** is the slope, and (0, **b**) is the y-intercept.
2. Plot **m** as a ratio ($\frac{\text{change in } y}{\text{change in } x}$).
3. Write (0, **b**).
4. Start at (0, **b**). Count up for positive change in y or down for negative change in y. Count over for the change in x—to the right if positive, to the left if negative.
5. Plot the point and draw the line.

$x + 3y = 6$

1. $y = \frac{^-x}{3} + 2$

2. Plot **b** = (0, 2)

3. $\mathbf{m} = \frac{^-1}{3}$

4. Count down 1 and to the right 3.

5. Plot the point and draw the line.

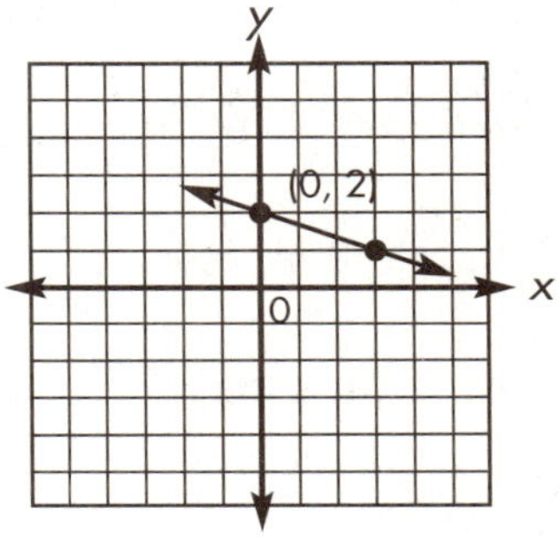

Directions: Use the slope-intercept form to graph each equation. Then use words to describe the line.

1. $y = 2x - 1$

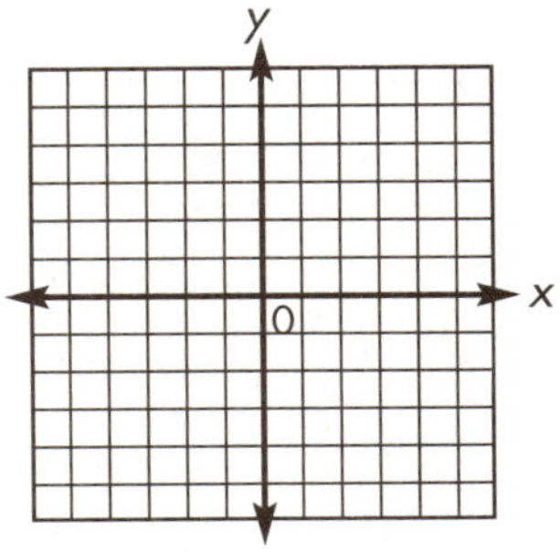

2. $2y = x - 4$

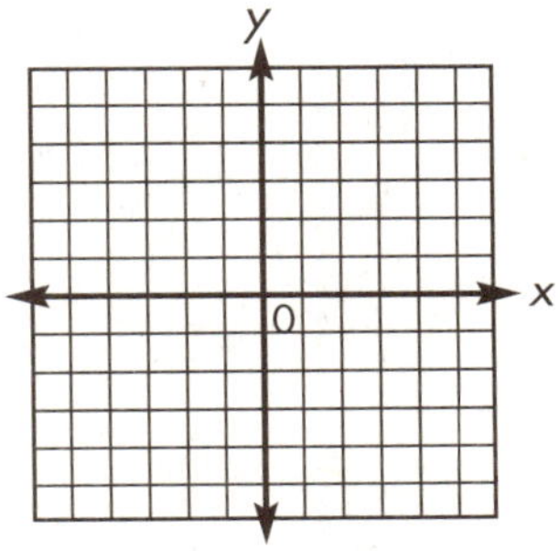

3. $y + x = 1$

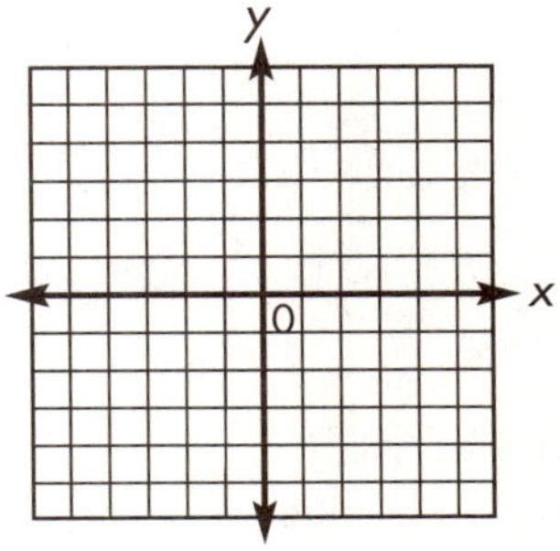

4. $2y = 3x + 6$

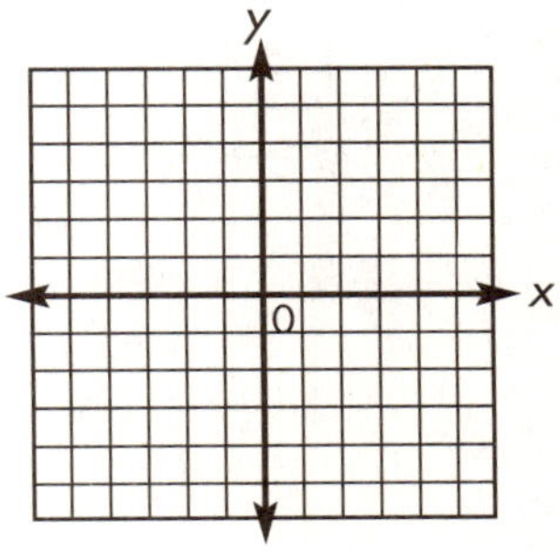

0-7696-4038-9 *Problem Solving*

Name ____________________ Date __________

Graphing Linear Equations

Directions: In the linear equation $y = \mathbf{m}x + \mathbf{b}$, **m** is the slope of the line and **b** is the y-intercept. Match each clue to its correct equation and graph. Write the letters on the lines.

Clue:	Equation	Graph
1. Slope is greater than 3. *Y*-intercept is negative.	______	______
2. Slope is a negative integer. *Y*-intercept is above the x-axis.	______	______
3. Slope is positive. *Y*-intercept is the origin.	______	______
4. Slope is less than $^{-}3$. *Y*-intercept is negative.	______	______
5. Slope is 0. *Y*-intercept is even.	______	______
6. Slope is between 0 and 1. *Y*-intercept is less than 0.	______	______
7. Slope is between $^{-}1$ and 0. *Y*-intercept is prime.	______	______
8. Slope is $^{-}1$. *Y*-intercept is 0.	______	______

Equations

A. $y = 2x$

B. $y = 2$

C. $y = -\frac{1}{2}x + 3$

D. $y = {^{-}4}x - 3$

E. $y = 4x - 3$

F. $y = \frac{1}{2}x - 3$

G. $y = {^{-}x}$

H. $y = {^{-}3}x + 2$

Graphs

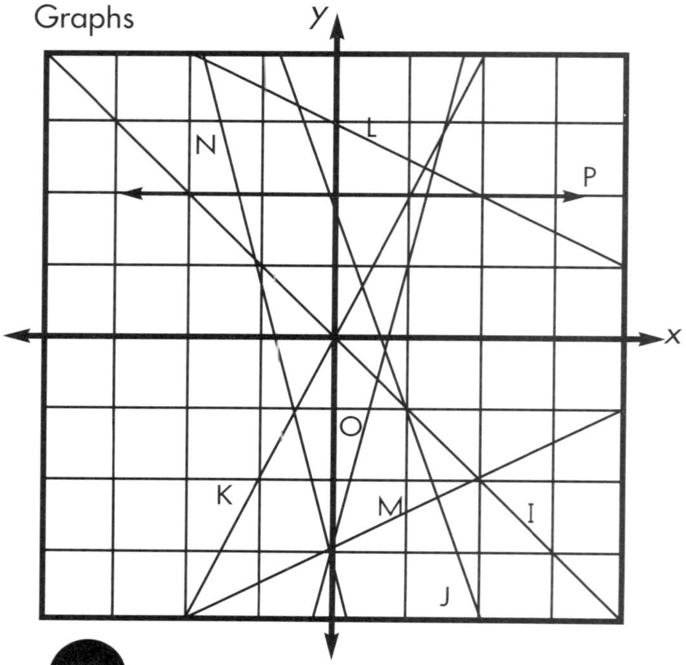

0-7696-4038-9 *Problem Solving*

Name ______________________ Date ____________

Parallel and Perpendicular Lines

Parallel lines never intersect. **Perpendicular** lines meet at a right angle.

Directions: Complete the tables and graph the equations.

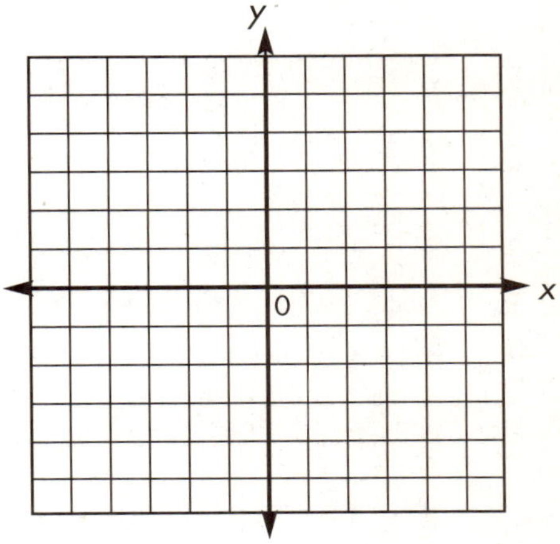

1. $y = 3x - 4$

x	y
0	$^-4$
1	
2	

2. $y = 3x - 1$

x	y
0	$^-1$
1	
2	

3. $y = x - 4$

x	y
0	$^-4$
1	
2	

4. What do equations 1 and 2 have in common? How does this make the graphs look?

____

____

5. What do equations 1 and 3 have in common? How does this make the graphs look?

____

____

Complete the tables and graph the equations.

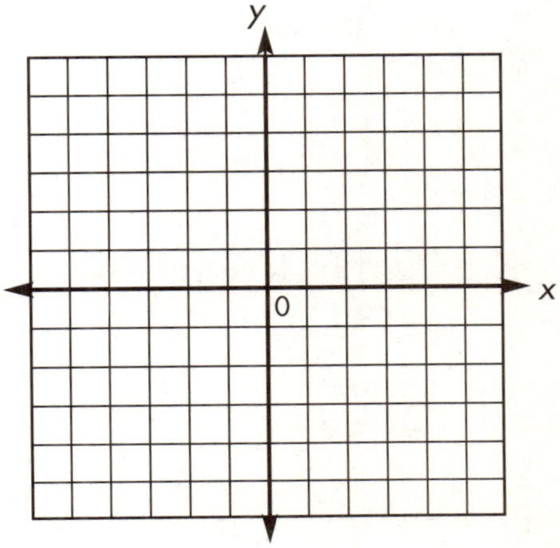

6. $y = (\frac{2}{3})x + 1$

x	y
0	1
3	
6	

7. $y = (\frac{^-3}{2})x + 1$

x	y
0	1
2	
4	

8. Compare the graphs for equations 6 and 7.

____

9. Compare equations 6 and 7.

____

Name ____________________ Date __________

Check Your Skills–Algebra

1. Mary sees a suit she would like to buy. It is priced at $90.00. Being a thrifty shopper, she decides to wait until it goes on sale. Three months later it appears one Monday morning on a clearance rack marked 10% discount. Mary knows that Tuesday the sale price from Monday will be reduced by 20%, and so on. If Mary holds off until the suit is under $20.00, on what day will she buy it? Create a chart and show all of your work to support your answer.

2. Look at the following sequence of numbers:

$1, 4, {}^{-}1, 6, {}^{-}3,$ ____, $^{-}5, 10, {}^{-}7, 12, {}^{-}9, 14, {}^{-}11, 16, {}^{-}13,$ ____, ____, ____, $^{-}17$

What strategies would you use to discover the pattern in the number sequence? Write down the strategy you think will be most effective and explain why. Then use that strategy to try to figure out the pattern. How can you discover if you've found the correct pattern?

3. On Earth a baseball player can throw a ball 280 ft. On Mars he can throw it 3 times as far as he can on Earth, but on Jupiter he can throw it $\frac{2}{5}$ as far. How far can he throw a ball on Mars? How far can he throw it on Jupiter? Assign variables and solve to find the answer.

4. Describe how you can find the slope and *y*-intercept of a line, using the equation shown below. Without graphing, how can you tell if the line will have a positive or negative slope?

$^{-}2x + y = 5$

0-7696-4038-9 *Problem Solving*

Name ______________________ Date __________

Classifying Angles

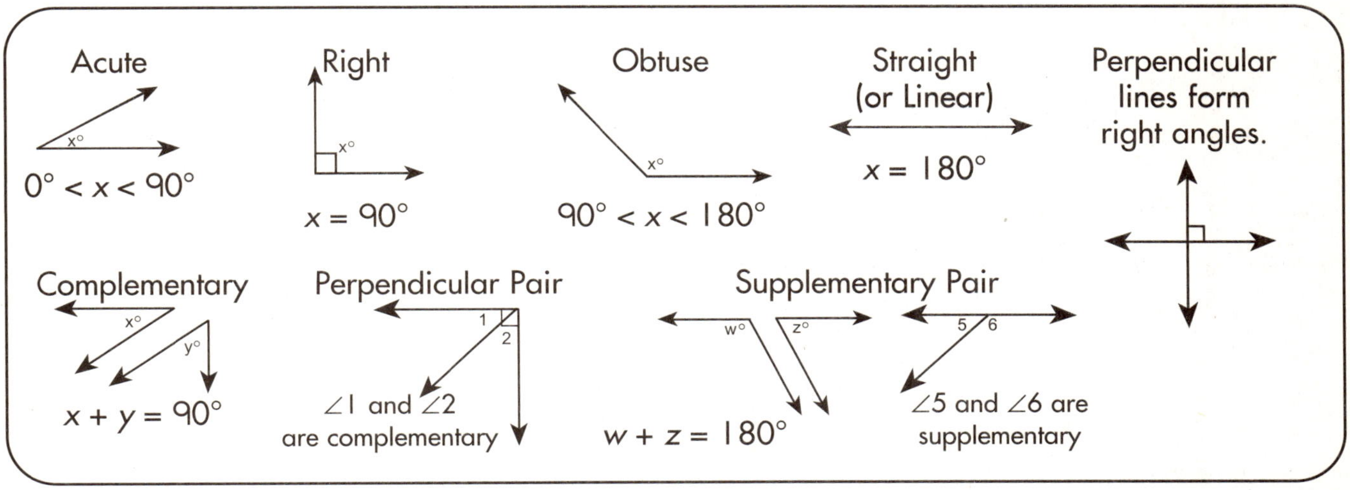

Directions: Find the angle measures for each situation below.

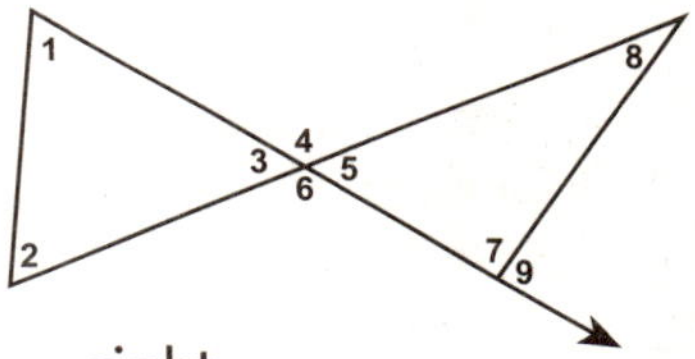

In the figure, $m\angle 7 = 90°$

1. Name the angles that appear to be:
   a. acute ____________ **b.** obtuse ____________ **c.** right ____________

2. Name five pairs of supplementary angles. ______________________________

3. $\angle 7$ and $\angle 9$ form a ______________________.

$\angle 10$ and $\angle 11$ are complementary angles.

4. $m\angle 10 = 32°$; $m\angle 11 =$ ______

5. $m\angle 11 = 72°$; $m\angle 10 =$ ______

6. $m\angle 10 = 4x$; $m\angle 11 = 2x$; $x =$ ______

7. $m\angle 10 = x$; $m\angle 11 = x + 20$; $x =$ ______

$\angle 12$ and $\angle 13$ are supplementary angles.

8. $m\angle 12 = 2y$; $m\angle 13 = 3y - 15$; $y =$ ______

9. $m\angle 12 = y + 10$; $m\angle 13 = 3y + 10$; $y =$ ______

10. The measure of $\angle 12$ is five times the measure of $\angle 13$. Find the measure of each angle.

$\angle 13$ and $\angle 14$ are complementary angles, and $\angle 14$ and $\angle 15$ are supplementary angles.

11. $m\angle 13 = 47°$; $m\angle 14 =$ ______; $m\angle 15 =$ ______

12. $m\angle 14 = 78°$; $m\angle 13 =$ ______; $m\angle 15 =$ ______

13. $m\angle 15 = 135°$; $m\angle 13 =$ ______; $m\angle 14 =$ ______

REFLECTING

What kinds of real-life careers utilize angle relationships?

0-7696-4038-9 *Problem Solving*

Name ______________________ Date ___________

Mixed Practice with Angles

Hatch marks indicate congruent parts.

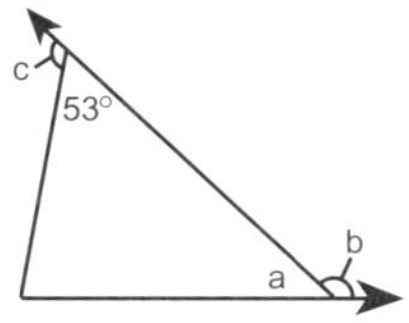

c = 180 – 53 = **127°**
b = c = **127°**
a = 180 – b = 180 – 127 = **53°**

Directions: Find the measure of the lettered angles.

1.

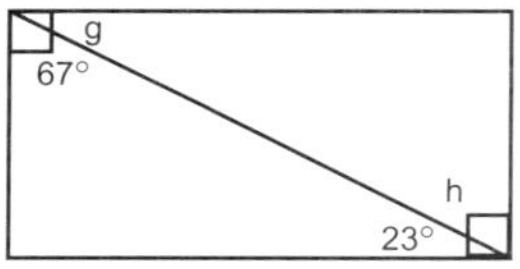

g = __________
h = __________

2.

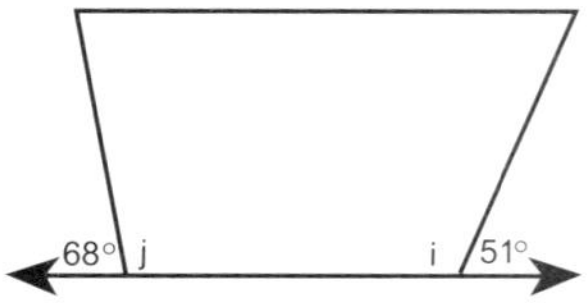

i = __________
j = __________

3.

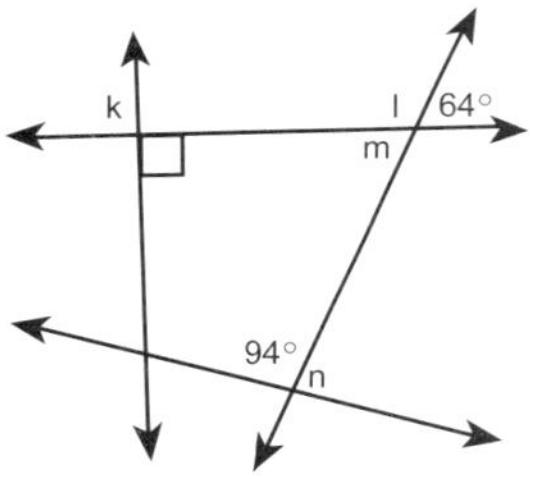

k = __________
l = __________
m = __________
n = __________

4.

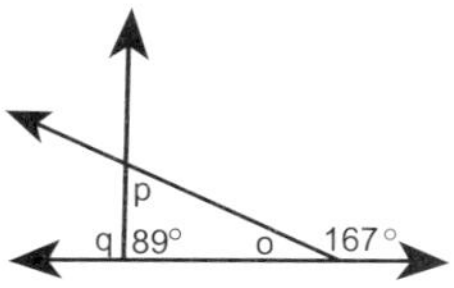

o = __________
p = __________
q = __________

5.

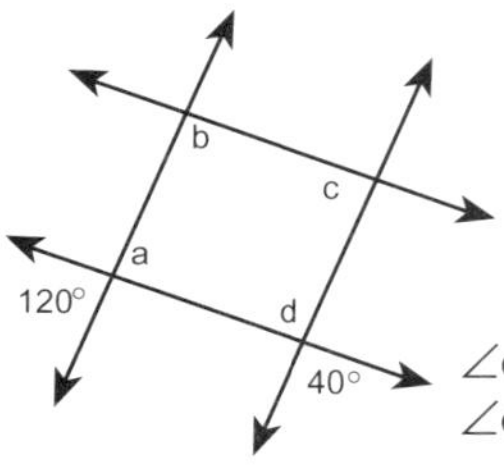

a = __________
b = __________
c = __________

∠a is supplementary to ∠b
∠c is supplementary to ∠d

6.

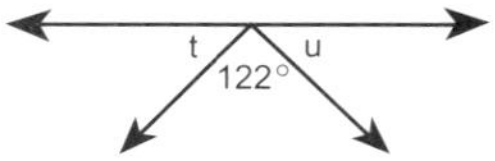

∠t ≅ ∠u
t = __________
u = __________

7.

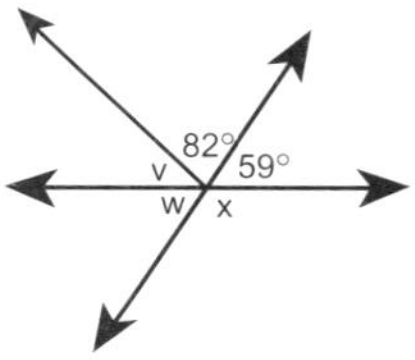

v = __________
w = __________
x = __________

8.

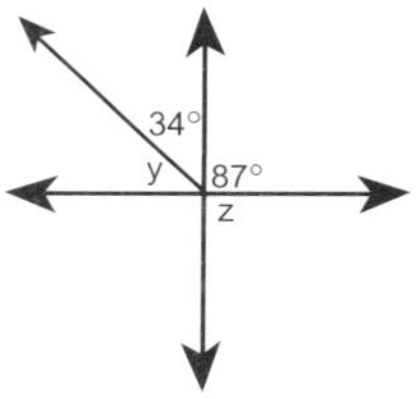

y = __________
z = __________

9.

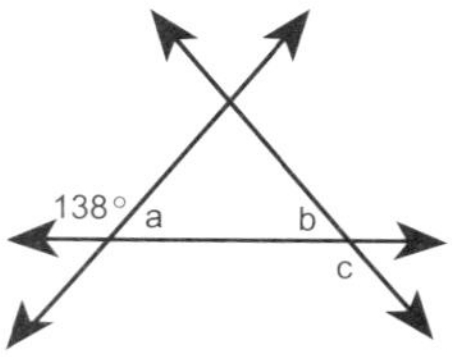

a = __________
b = __________
c = __________

∠a is complementary to ∠b

10.

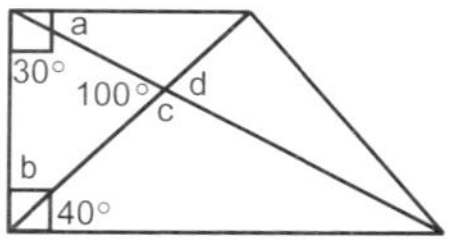

a = __________
b = __________
c = __________
d = __________

EXTENDING

Draw a series of intersecting lines. Assign letters and one measurement to the angles formed from the intersections. Exchange drawings with a classmate and calculate the missing measures.

0-7696-4038-9 *Problem Solving*

Name ______________________ Date ____________

Angles and Parallel Lines

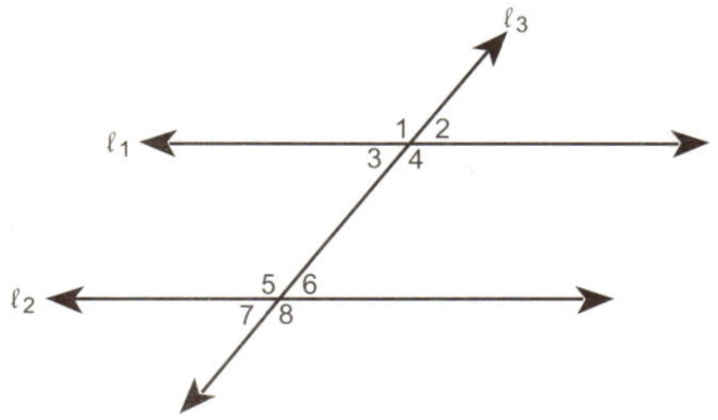

ℓ_1 and ℓ_2 are **parallel lines** (they do not intersect).
ℓ_3 is a **transversal.**

Eight angles are formed:
vertical angles = ∠1 & ∠4, ∠2 & ∠3, ∠5 & ∠8, ∠6 & ∠7
interior angles = ∠3, ∠4, ∠5, and ∠6
same side interior angles = ∠3 & ∠4, ∠5 & ∠6
alternate side interior angles = ∠3 & ∠6, ∠4 & ∠5
exterior angles = ∠1, ∠2, ∠7, and ∠8
same side exterior angles = ∠1 & ∠7, ∠2 & ∠8
alternate side exterior angles = ∠1 & ∠8, ∠2 & ∠7
corresponding angles = ∠1 & ∠5, ∠2 & ∠6, ∠3 & ∠7, ∠4 & ∠8

Directions: Given two parallel lines, same side interior angles are supplementary. Fill in the blanks with the correct answers.

1. Vertical angles are ____.
2. Same side exterior angles are ______________________________________.
3. Alternate side interior angles are ___________________________________.
4. Alternate side exterior angles are ___________________________________.
5. Corresponding angles are ____.
6. Find the measures of the designated angles. ℓ_1 is parallel to ℓ_2.

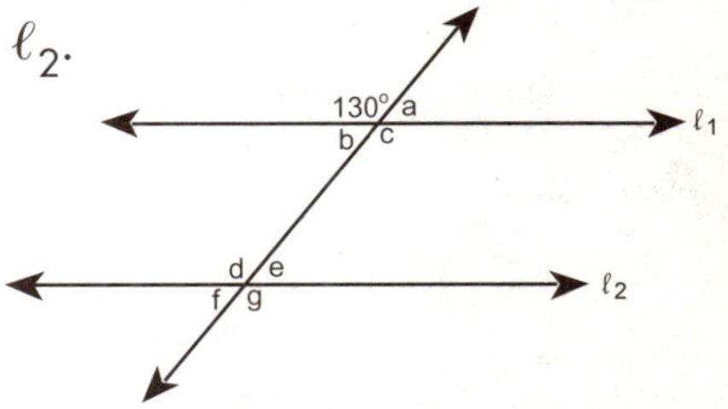

a. m∠a = ________ **e.** m∠e = ________
b. m∠b = ________ **f.** m∠f = ________
c. m∠c = ________ **g.** m∠g = ________
d. m∠d = ________

7. Examine the diagram on the right. Given that a ∥ b and c ∥ d, find the measures for angles 1 through 15. Write out how you know your answers are correct. Use the correct names for the angles from the example box above.

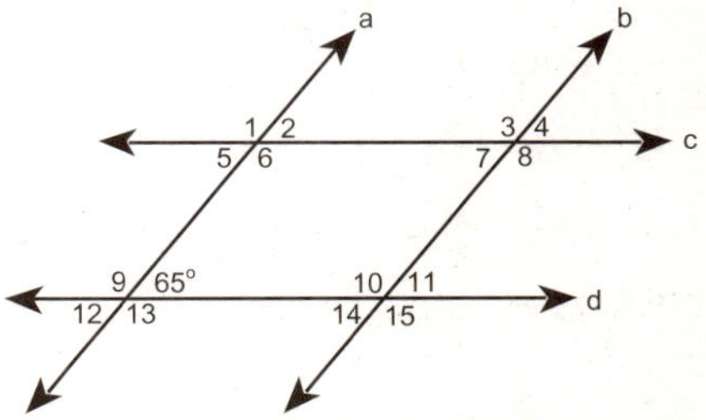

0-7696-4038-9 *Problem Solving*

Name ______________________ Date __________

More Angles and Parallel Lines

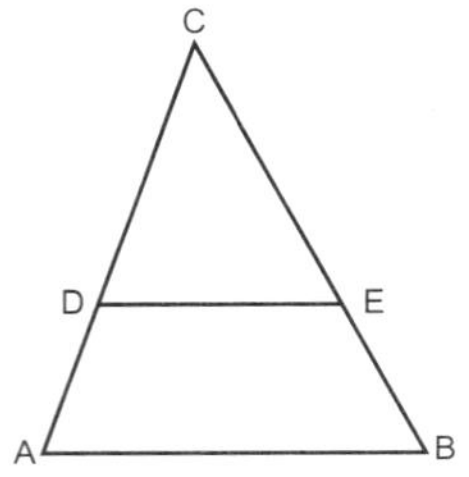

$\overline{AB} \parallel \overline{DE}$, $\angle A = 60°$, $m\angle B = 50°$

$60 + 50 + m\angle C = 180°$
$m\angle C = 70°$

$m\angle CDE = 60°$
$\angle CDE \cong \angle CAB$

$60 + m\angle EDA = 180°$
$m\angle EDA = 120°$

Directions: Find the missing values.

1. $\overline{AD} \parallel \overline{EG}$, $\overline{EC} \parallel \overline{FD}$,
$\overline{EG} \perp \overline{AE}$, $m\angle CBA = 140°$

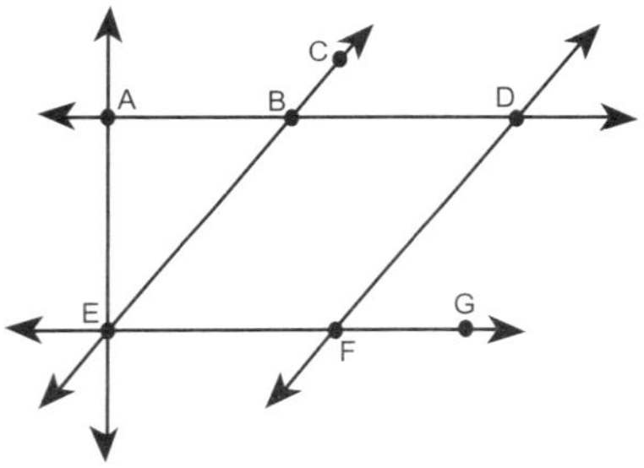

a. $m\angle ABE$ = __________
b. $m\angle EAB$ = __________
c. $m\angle AEB$ = __________
d. $m\angle BEF$ = __________
e. $m\angle EFD$ = __________
f. $m\angle BDF$ = __________
g. $m\angle DFG$ = __________

2. $\overline{AC} \parallel \overline{DF}$, $\overline{AD} \parallel \overline{BE} \parallel \overline{CF}$, $\overline{BD} \parallel \overline{CE}$,
$\overline{AE} \parallel \overline{BF}$, $m\angle BDE = 30°$, $m\angle ADB = 20°$,
$m\angle BEG = 70°$

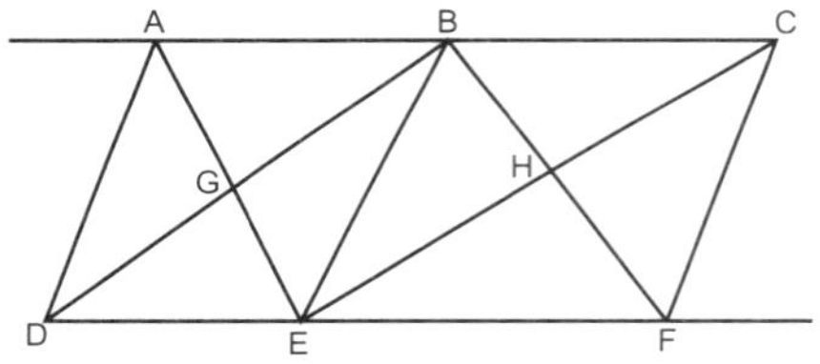

a. $m\angle BAD$ = __________
b. $m\angle BAE$ = __________
c. $m\angle ABD$ = __________
d. $m\angle AGB$ = __________
e. $m\angle BED$ = __________
f. $m\angle BEF$ = __________
g. $m\angle BFE$ = __________

3. $\overline{MN} \parallel \overline{RS}$, $\overline{MO} \parallel \overline{NR} \parallel \overline{QS}$, $\overline{OR} \parallel \overline{MS} \parallel \overline{NQ}$,
$m\angle NMP = 75°$, $m\angle RPS = 40°$

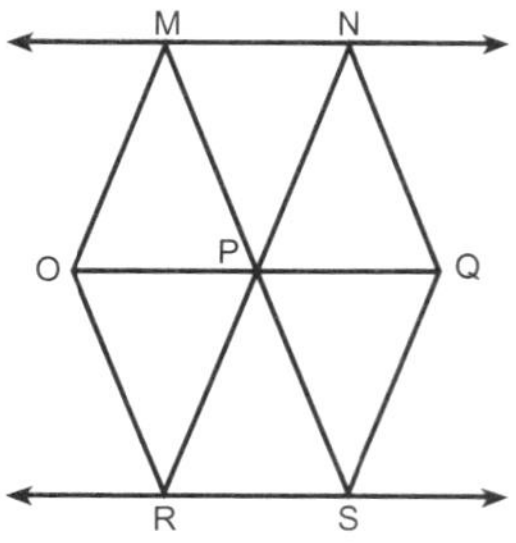

a. $m\angle MNP$ = __________
b. $m\angle MPN$ = __________
c. $m\angle PMO$ = __________
d. $m\angle MOP$ = __________
e. $m\angle OPM$ = __________
f. $m\angle OPR$ = __________

Name ______________________ Date ____________

Parts of a Circle

Directions: Write the letter of each term next to the corresponding part of the circle. Some terms may be used more than once.

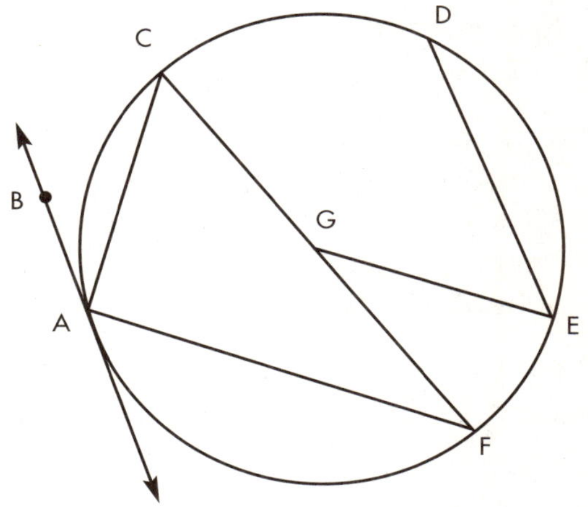

_____ **1.** $\overset{\frown}{AF}$

_____ **2.** $\overline{AF}$

_____ **3.** $\overset{\frown}{CD}$

_____ **4.** $\overline{CG}$

_____ **5.** $\overset{\frown}{CDF}$

_____ **6.** $\overline{CF}$

_____ **7.** $\angle EGF$

_____ **8.** $\overset{\frown}{ACF}$

_____ **9.** $\overleftrightarrow{AB}$

_____ **10.** $\overline{AC}$

_____ **11.** $\overset{\frown}{AEC}$

_____ **12.** $\angle CAF$

_____ **13.** $\angle GED$

_____ **14.** G

_____ **15.** $\overset{\frown}{CAF}$

_____ **16.** $\overline{GF}$

A. center

B. chord

C. diameter

D. radius

E. tangent

F. semicircle

G. minor arc

H. major arc

I. central angle

J. inscribed angle

EXTENDING

Draw a circle with a center, a tangent, a diameter, radii, and chords. Label the parts of your circle. Then try to describe the circle to a classmate without the classmate seeing your drawing. While you use the correct vocabulary words to explain where the different parts are located, have your classmate try to draw your circle. Compare your original circle and your classmate's version. Then switch roles.

0-7696-4038-9 *Problem Solving*

Name ______________________ Date __________

Arc to Arcturus

Materials needed: protractor

An **arc** is part of a circle. The degree measure of an arc is the measure of its **central angle**. A central angle cuts a circle into two arcs. The arc less than a semicircle is the **minor arc** and is named by its endpoints, $\overset{\frown}{AB}$. The arc greater than a semicircle is the **major arc**. A third point is needed to name the major arc, $\overset{\frown}{ACB}$.

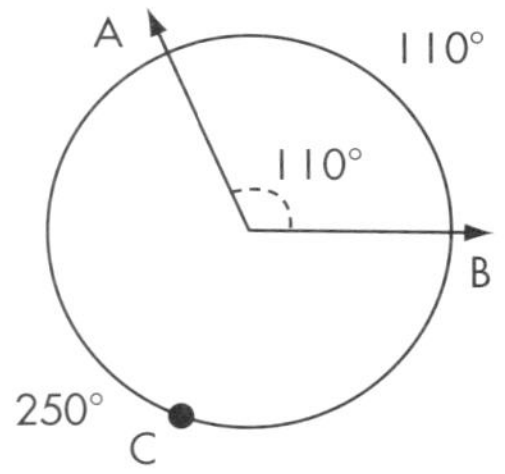

Directions: Use a protractor to find the arc degree measure associated with each sector of the circle graph.

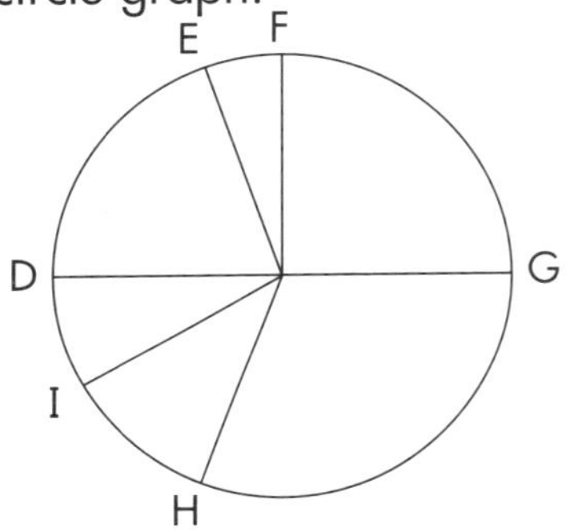

1. $\overset{\frown}{DE}$ __________

2. $\overset{\frown}{FG}$ __________

3. $\overset{\frown}{HI}$ __________

4. $\overset{\frown}{EF}$ __________

5. $\overset{\frown}{GH}$ __________

6. $\overset{\frown}{ID}$ __________

7. The sum of the answers to #1–6 is __________.

An **inscribed angle** has the vertex on the circle, and both rays intersect the circle. The inscribed angle XYZ determines the same arc as the central angle XWZ.

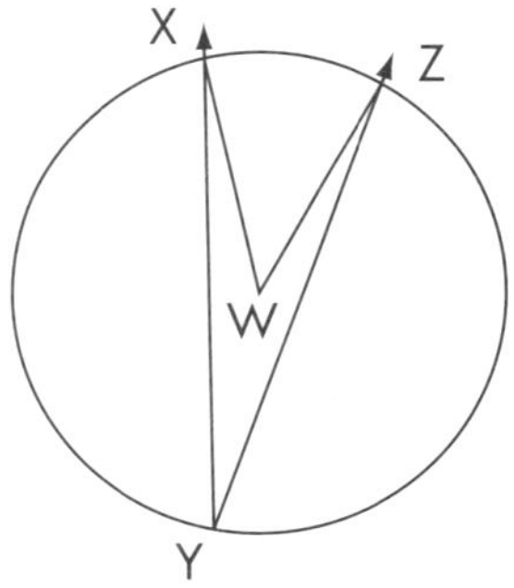

8. Measure angle XYZ. __________

9. How does angle XYZ compare to angle XWZ? __________

10. If an inscribed angle PQR = 40°, what is the measure of minor arc PR? __________

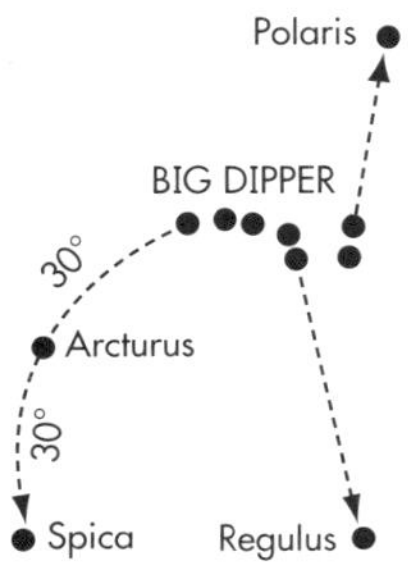

In the night sky you can locate the star Arcturus by following the arc of the handle of the Big Dipper 30°. Another 30° arc locates the star Spica.

11. If the arc distance from the Big Dipper to Arcturus measures 2 cm on a picture, the full circle would have a circumference of __________ cm.

12. The Big Dipper to Spica arc is what part of a full circle? __________

0-7696-4038-9 *Problem Solving*

Name ______________________ Date ____________

A Triangle Formula

Materials needed: graph paper, tracing paper, straightedge, protractor

A **right triangle** has one 90 degree angle

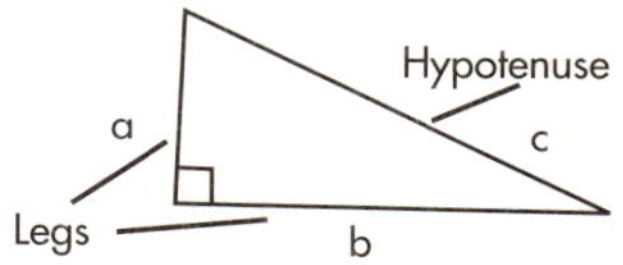

Directions: Follow the directions to develop a triangle formula.

1. Use graph paper. Each square on the graph paper is 1 square unit. Draw the legs of a right triangle. Use the lengths given in the table. Then draw the hypotenuse by connecting the legs.

2. For each triangle draw a square along each of its sides, like the drawing shown here. You may want to use tracing paper and a protractor to help make a perfect square along the edge of the hypotenuse. Label the squares 1, 2, and 3. Square 3 is always the square made from the hypotenuse.

Leg 1	Leg 2
1	2
2	2
3	4
6	8

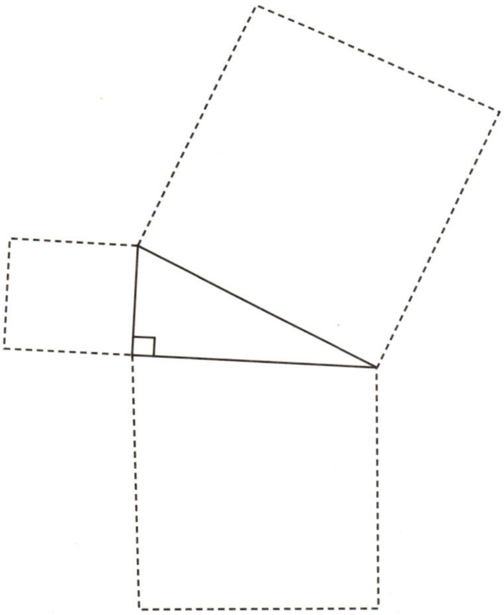

3. Find the area of squares 1 and 2 by counting each square unit. Estimate the area of square 3. Record your answers in the table below.

Square 1	Square 2	Square 3

Name ____________________ Date __________

A Triangle Formula (cont.)

4. Find a relationship between the areas of squares 1, 2, and 3. Describe the relationship.

5. Draw a right triangle. Label the lengths of the legs *a* and *b*. Label the hypotenuse *c*. Sketch squares along each side of the triangle. Label the squares A, B, and C to correspond to the side lengths.

a. Write an expression showing how to find the area of square A. ________________

b. Write an expression showing how to find the area of square B. ________________

c. Write an expression showing how to find the area of square C. ________________

6. Write an equation showing the relationship between the side lengths *a*, *b*, and *c* of a right triangle. ______________________________

7. Use the equation you wrote in problem 6 to help you find the length of each missing side.

a.

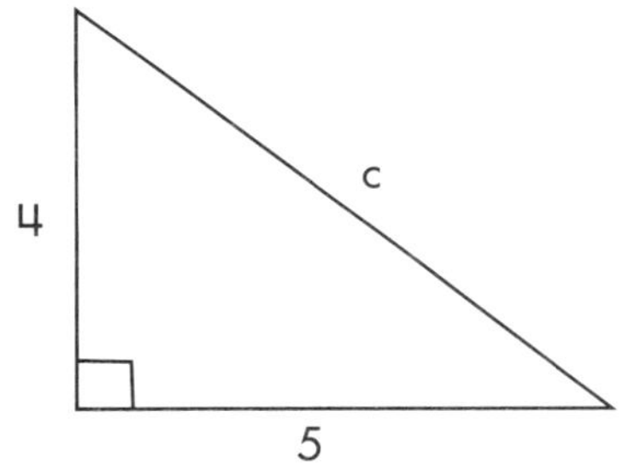

b.

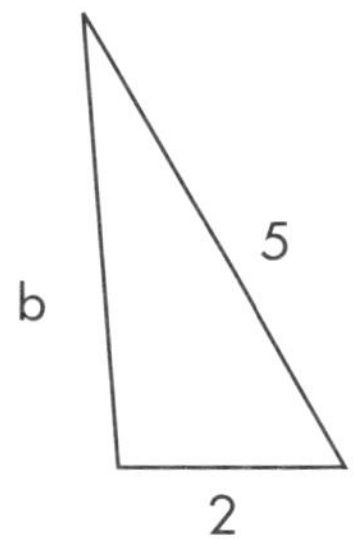

EXTENDING

The equation you wrote in problem 6 is called the Pythagorean theorem. Use that equation to figure out the following problem.

Isabel likes the plans for her family's new home, except for the triangular room on the second floor. On the plans the room resembles the diagram shown. What would Isabel find incorrect about the plan for this room? Explain your answer in words and numbers.

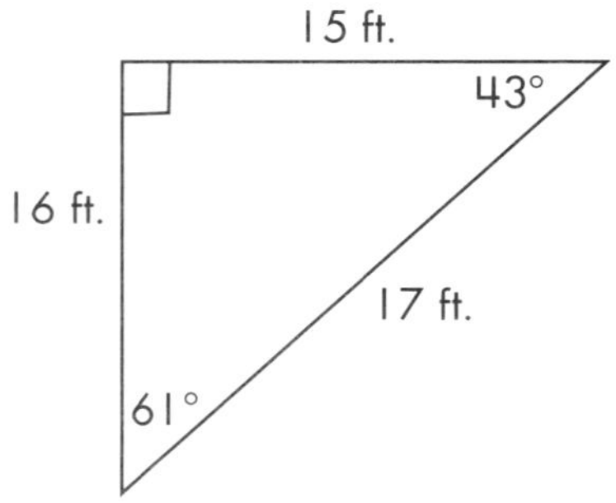

0-7696-4038-9 *Problem Solving*

Name ____________________ Date __________

Perimeter and Circumference

The **perimeter** of a regular or irregular polygon is the distance around its outside edges. That distance is found by computing the sum of its sides.

The **circumference** of a circle can be likened to the perimeter of a polygon. The formula for circumference is $C = \pi d$, or $C = 2\pi r$.

Directions: Compute the perimeter or circumference of each figure.

1. A rectangle with a long side of 24 cm and a short side of 14 cm __________

2. A hexagon with sides of $3\frac{3}{4}$ in. __________

3. A circle with a diameter of 60 m __________

4. A rectangle that is 120 ft. on one side and $20\frac{1}{3}$ yd. on the other side __________

5. A pentagon with all sides 3.5 inches __________

Solve the problems involving perimeter and circumference.

6. Trey made a large circular region using a rope. The region has a diameter of $12\frac{2}{3}$ ft. How many feet of rope did Trey have available?

7. Janelle is building a pen to house her rabbits. The pen will be rectangular and will have the back of the barn as one of its longer sides. Janelle has planned to have 180 sq. ft. of space within the pen, with the short sides of the pen each measuring 6 ft. How much fencing material will she need?

8. Sharon is building a circular brick path in her garden. Sharon knows the project will take four weekends to finish since she can complete only one section of the walkway at a time. The circular path will have a diameter of 40 ft. once it is completed. How many feet of walkway should Sharon be able to finish the first weekend?

0-7696-4038-9 *Problem Solving*

Name ______________________ Date __________

Area

Area is a measure of the size of a surface or of a flat expanse.
Several formulas are shown below.

Rectangle (includes squares): A = length x width
$A = lw$

Triangle: $A = \frac{1}{2}$ x base x height
$A = \frac{1}{2}bh$

Circle: $A = \pi r^2$

Directions: Compute the area for each of the regular figures described below. Draw a diagram for each situation. Use a calculator to check your answers.

1. A rectangle with sides of 20 in. and 40 in. __________

2. A square with sides of 7 cm __________

3. A triangle with a base of $3\frac{1}{2}$ in. and a height of $6\frac{1}{4}$ in. __________

4. A circle with a radius of 6 m __________

5. Find the portion of a 16-in. by 16-in. square that is not covered by a circle. The circle has a radius of 3 in. and has been placed in the center of the square.

0-7696-4038-9 *Problem Solving*

Name ____________________ Date __________

Area (cont.)

6. Find the total area formed by a triangle with a base of $4\frac{1}{4}$ in. and a height of 10 in. and a rectangle that is 10 in. by $4\frac{1}{4}$ in.

7. Rakeem has staked out a rectangular region for planting a garden. The region is 50 ft. long by $12\frac{1}{2}$ ft. wide. He plans to use one-fifth of the garden's overall area for flowers. How many square feet of garden will he use for flowers?

8. Acme-Ace Garage Parking Facility has three levels available for parked cars. Each level is rectangular in shape and measures 220 ft. by 80 ft. On each level, 22.5% of the available area is used for ramps, driveways, and other special zones. How much floor space does Acme-Ace have available for parking vehicles?

9. The tin roof of Carolyn's vacation house was damaged. The roof is composed of two large sections that are rectangular in shape and adjoin at the roof peak. Each of these two large sections measures 60 ft. by 36 ft.

a. What is the total area of the roof on Carolyn's vacation house? __________

b. The piece of her roof that was damaged and needs replacing measures 3 ft. by 12 ft. What percentage of the whole roof does this piece represent? __________

10. A teacher has decided that the circular-shaped parachute used for recess should be trimmed and resewn. The parachute is currently 60 ft. in diameter. She plans to trim $1\frac{1}{2}$ ft. off the outside edge all the way around. What will be the area of this parachute once it has been trimmed? __________

Name ______________________ Date __________

Area Challenges

Directions: Use a variety of strategies to find the missing information in each problem. Explain how you found each answer.

1. Avis Starr, a famous actress and the town's wealthiest resident, had a new pool built in the backyard of her mansion. If the pool is shaped as below, how many square feet of material will she need for her custom-made pool cover?

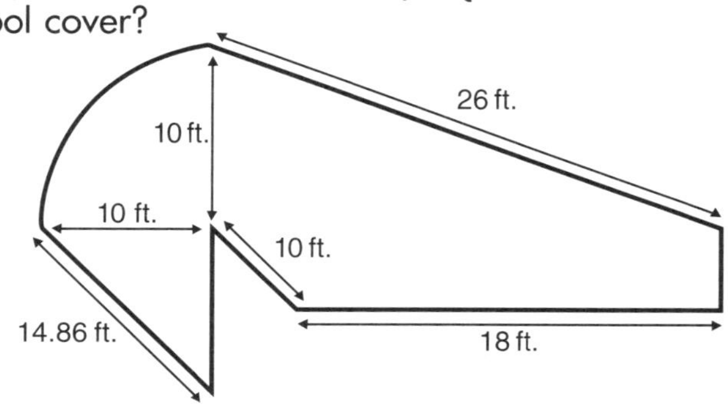

2. Flickering Middle School is planning to resurface its 440-yd. track with artificial turf. If the dimensions of the track are as shown, how much artificial turf will be needed to cover the track surface?

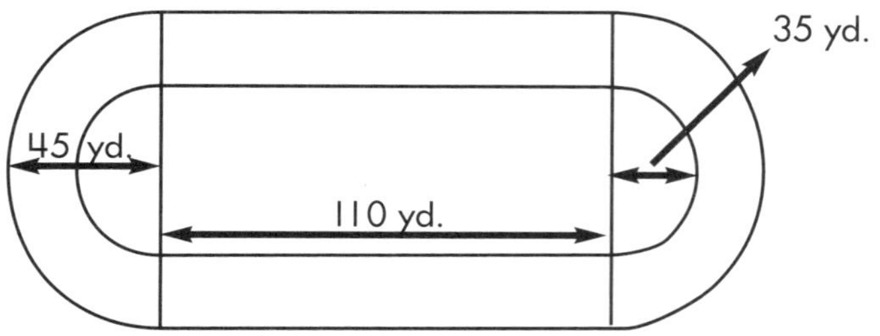

3. The school's new soccer balls are covered with 64 regular hexagonal panels. Each hexagon measures 2 in. between opposite corners and 1.5 in. between opposite sides. What is the total surface area of the soccer ball?

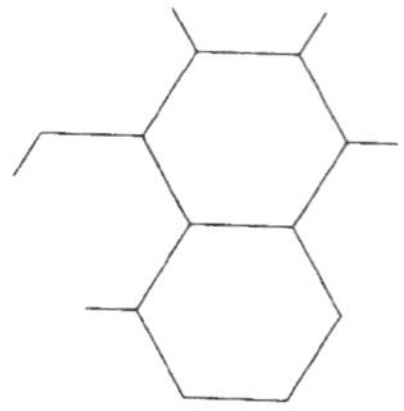

4. The longer base of a trapezoid is the square of the shorter base. The nonparallel sides are congruent. Each nonparallel side is 4 more than the shorter base. If the perimeter of the trapezoid is 36, what are the lengths of each base and the sides? Include a diagram with your answer.

0-7696-4038-9 *Problem Solving*

Name ______________________ Date __________

Volume

Imagine the inside of an enclosed space such as a traffic cone, a cardboard box, or one of the ancient pyramids of Egypt. The interior space of an object is its **volume**. The volumes of many standard figures may be easily found using formulas.

Rectangular Prism (including cubes):
$V = \text{length} \times \text{width} \times \text{height}$
$V = lwh$

Square or Rectangular Pyramid:
$V = \frac{1}{3} \times (\text{area of base}) \times \text{height}$
$V = \frac{1}{3} \times (l \times w) \times h$
$V = \frac{1}{3} lwh$

Cylinder:
$V = (\text{area of base}) \times \text{height}$
$V = \pi r^2 \times h$
$V = \pi r^2 h$

Cone:
$V = \frac{1}{3} (\text{area of base}) \times \text{height}$
$V = \frac{1}{3} (\pi r^2) \times h$
$V = \frac{1}{3} \pi r^2 h$

Sphere:
$V = \frac{4}{3} \pi r^2$

Directions: Compute the volume for each of the regular figures described below.

1. A rectangular prism with a height of 3 cm, a width of 3 cm, and a length of 12 cm ________

2. A square pyramid with a base of 6 in. by 6 in. and a height of 6 in. ________

3. A cylinder with a height of 40 cm and a radius of 5 cm ________

4. A cone-shaped water cup with a height of 12 cm and a radius of 8 cm ________

5. A rectangular-shaped storage shed with interior dimensions of 12 ft. by 8 ft. by 8 ft. ________

0-7696-4038-9 *Problem Solving*

Name ____________________ Date __________

Volume (cont.)

Rewrite each of the volume-related formulas into a simplified algebraic form, depending on the figures involved.

6. The formula of a rectangular prism changed to describe only a cube with sides of q.
____

7. The formula of a pyramid changed to describe only a square-based pyramid with sides of y.
____

8. The formula of a cylinder changed to describe a cylinder whose height is the same measure as its radius. ____________________

9. The formula for the portion of a cylinder not occupied when a smaller cone is stored inside the cylinder. ____________________

Solve the volume-related problems below.

10. Griffin took a storage box with a height of 20 in. and cut off a 4-in. strip all the way around, thereby reducing the height of the box. If the box had been capable of holding 2,000 cu. in. of material before the strip was removed, how much can it now hold?

11. Priya is planning to move to a new apartment. She has the choice of buying a cylindrical container for packing dishes and glassware or buying a similarly sized rectangular box. The cylinder drum's interior is 40 inches tall with a radius of 11 inches. The box's interior is 36 inches tall with both a length and width of 24 inches. Which box has more storage space? by how much more?

12. Loo wants to buy a dishwasher. The problem is that the counter where it must be installed is only $32\frac{3}{4}$ in. deep. The dishwasher with the closest matching depth is $34\frac{1}{8}$ in. from back to front. Its height is 34 in., and its width is 30 in., both measures being within the limits of the space available. If installed, how many cubic inches of this dishwasher will stick out beyond the counter?

0-7696-4038-9 *Problem Solving*

Name ____________________ Date __________

Pyramids and Cones

Pyramids and **cones** are solids with one base and a major vertex.
The area (A) of a 2-dimensional triangle equals $\frac{1}{2}$ x base x height.
The volume (V) of a 3-dimensional pyramid is $\frac{1}{3}$ x area of the base (B) x height.

Directions: Use the formulas below to find the answer to each situation.

1. Compare $A = \frac{1}{2}bh$ and $V = \frac{1}{3}Bh$.

2. Find the volume of a square pyramid 6 ft. tall with a base 10 ft. on a side.

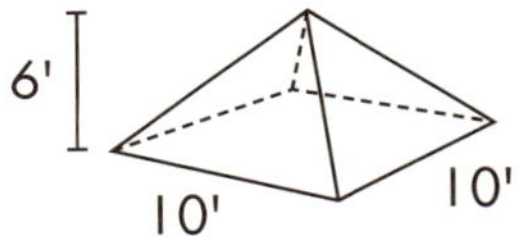

3. Find the volume of a square pyramid 10 ft. high with a base 6 ft. on a side.

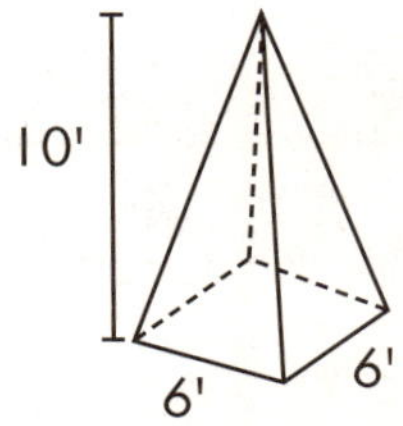

4. Find the volume of a triangular pyramid 10 ft. high with a base of 6 ft. and height of 8 ft.

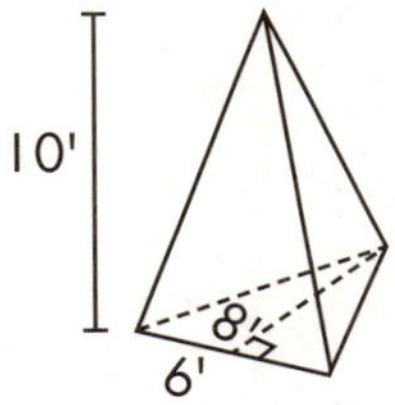

A cone has one circular base and a curved surface that connects the base to one vertex.
$V = \frac{1}{3}$ x area of the base x height or $V = \frac{1}{3}\pi r^2 h$. Let $\pi = \frac{22}{7}$.

5. A road-salt storage building is cone-shaped. Its height is 21 ft., and its base has a radius of 14 ft. How many cubic feet of salt will it hold?

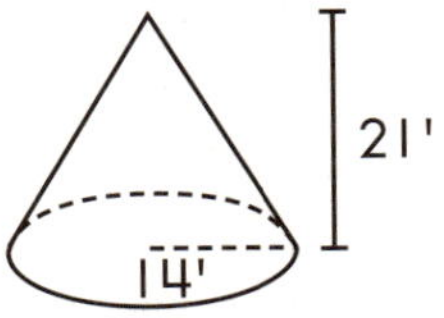

6. An ice-cream cone has a height of 7 cm and a base radius of 3 cm. Find the volume of the cone.

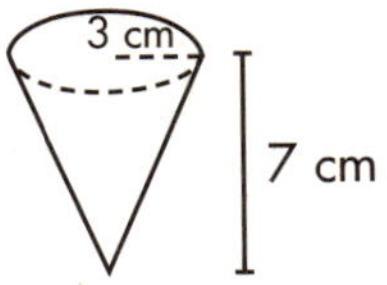

7. A truck has a trailer that measures 16 ft. long, 6 ft. wide, and 5 ft. high.

a. Find the volume of the trailer.

____

b. How many trailer loads will fill the storage building in problem 5?

____

8. The volume of a sphere = $\frac{4}{3} \times \pi r^3$.

a. Find the volume of a 3-cm (radius) sphere of ice cream. __________

b. If the ice cream melts, will it overflow the cone in problem 6?

____

0-7696-4038-9 *Problem Solving*

Name ______________________ Date __________

Similar Figures and Perimeter

In similar figures, the ratio of the perimeter is equal to the ratio of any pair of sides.

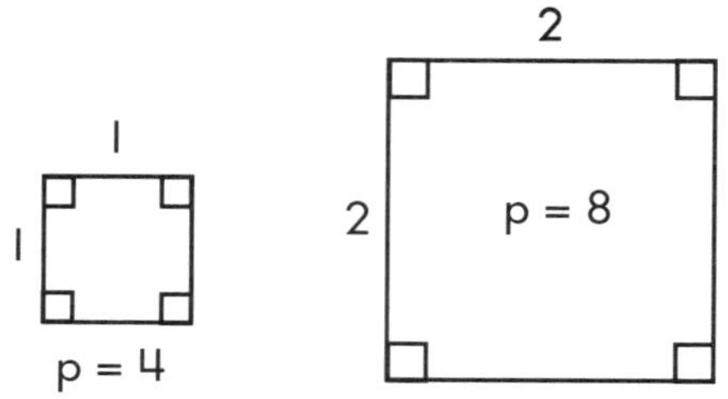

$\frac{1}{2}$ = sides ratio

$\frac{4}{8} = \frac{1}{2}$ = perimeter ratio

Directions: Find the missing perimeter, ratio, or labeled side. All figures are similar.

1.

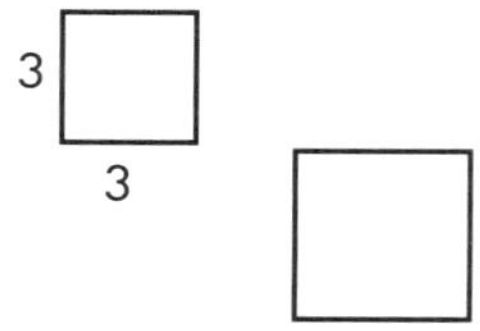

ratio = $\frac{2}{3}$

P = ________

2.

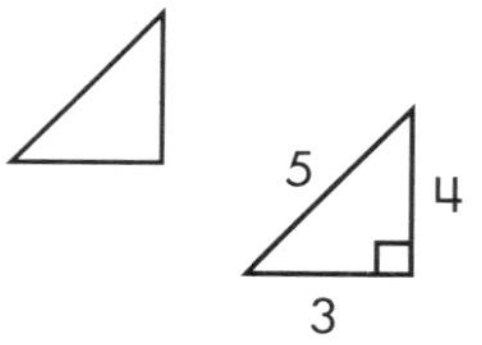

ratio = $\frac{3}{4}$

P = ________

3.

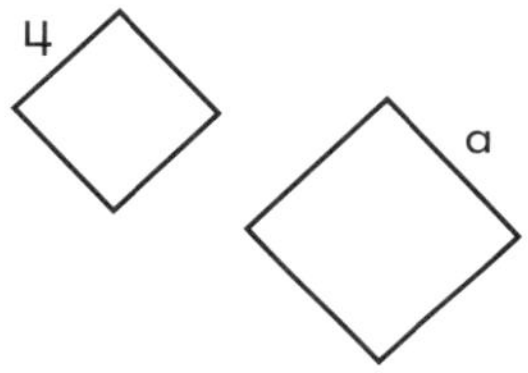

ratio = $\frac{2}{3}$

a = ________

4.

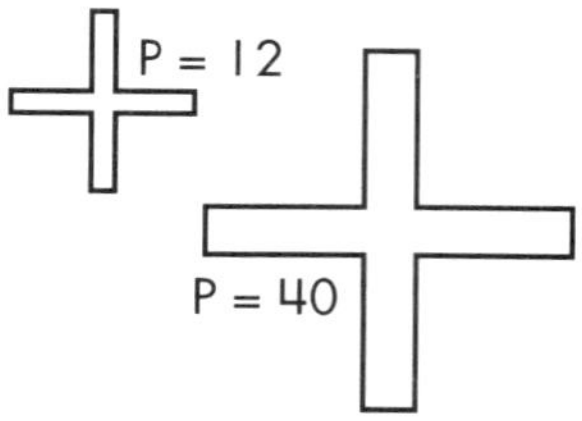

P = 12
P = 40

ratio =________

5.

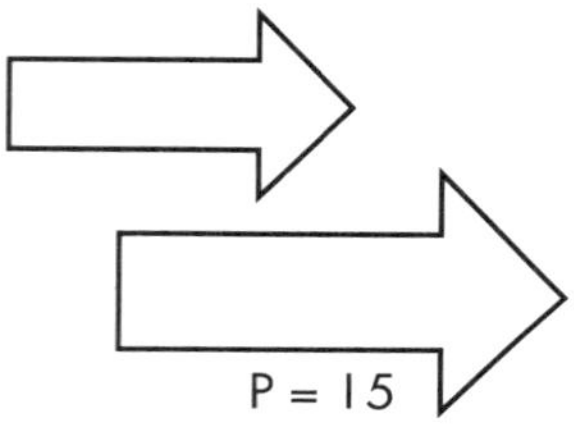

ratio = $\frac{3}{5}$

P = ________

6.

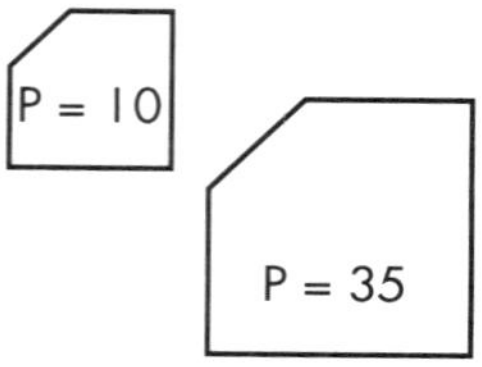

P = 10
P = 35

ratio =________

EXPLAINING

Draw two similar figures and assign one label. Explain to a classmate how to find the perimeters, ratios, and missing labeled sides.

Name ____________________ Date __________

More with Similar Figures

Materials needed: graph paper

Directions: Follow the directions for each similar-figure situation.

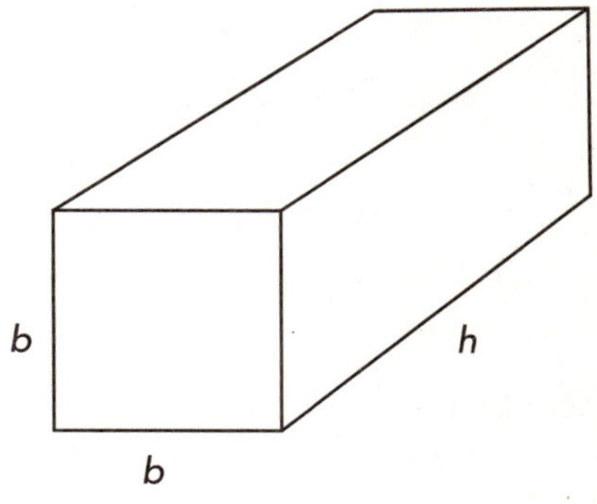

1. Imagine that all of the dimensions of a square prism have been doubled in length.

   a. What do you think will happen to the perimeter of each face?

   b. What do you think will happen to the surface area of the prism?

   c. What do you think will happen to the volume of the prism?

2. Draw a rectangular prism on another piece of paper. Decide what dimensions you want your prism to have. On a piece of graph paper, draw each face of the prism to scale. Every square on the graph paper represents 1 square unit.

   a. What are the dimensions of your prism?

      base length = __________ height = __________

   b. Find the perimeter of all of the faces of your prism. P = __________

   c. Find the surface area of your prism. A = __________

   d. Find the volume of your prism. V = __________

3. Double the dimensions of each edge of your prism.

   base length x 2 = __________ height x 2 = __________

   a. Draw your new prism on another piece of paper and label the dimensions.

   b. On a piece of graph paper, draw each face of the new prism to scale.

0-7696-4038-9 *Problem Solving*

Name ______________________ Date __________

More with Similar Figures (cont.)

c. Find the perimeter of all of the faces of your prism. P = ________

d. Find the surface area of your prism. A = ________

e. Find the volume of your prism. V = ________

4. Compare the perimeters, surface areas, and volumes of the two prisms. Be specific. Did the measurements change the way you thought they would? Why or why not?

5. What do you think will happen to the perimeter, surface area, and volume of a square prism if all of its side lengths are tripled?

6. Design and carry out a procedure to test your prediction in problem 5.

a. What happens to the perimeter of a prism if all of its side lengths are tripled?

b. What happens to the surface area of a prism if all of its side lengths are tripled?

c. What happens to the volume of a prism if all of its side lengths are tripled?

d. Were your predictions correct?

EXTENDING

In what kind of units are length, area, and volume measured? Explain how this relates to the way the perimeter, surface area, and volume of a prism change when the sides are increased by a scale factor of *k*.

Name ______________________ Date ___________

Similar Triangles

Directions: The two triangles shown here are similar. They have the same angle measurements. The side lengths are in proportion to one another. Respond to the items below to find the missing side lengths.

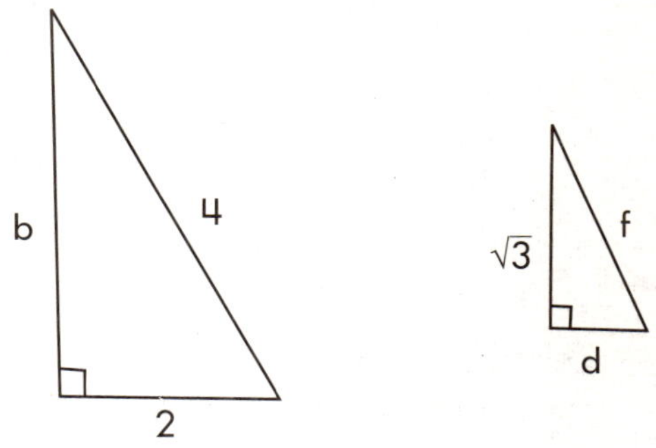

1. Mark the triangles to show which sides correspond to one another.

2. To find the scale factor between the triangles, you need to find a pair of corresponding sides whose measurements you know. Why is that difficult in this problem?

3. Answer the following questions to help you find the third side of the larger triangle.

a. What kind of triangle is this?

b. How does identifying the triangle type help? What do you know about the relationship between the three sides of the triangle?

c. Find the length of the missing side. Show your work.

4. Now look at both triangles and find a pair of corresponding sides whose measurements you know. What is the scale factor between the two triangles? Show your work.

5. Find the lengths of any remaining missing sides. Show your work.

EXPLAINING

Describe how to find the scale factor between two similar objects. Then tell how that scale factor can be used to find missing side lengths.

0-7696-4038-9 *Problem Solving*

Name ______________________ Date __________

Working with Similar Triangles

Corresponding angles of similar triangles are congruent. Corresponding sides are in proportion.

$\triangle ABC \sim \triangle DEF$

$m\angle A = m\angle D$, $m\angle B = m\angle E$, $m\angle C = m\angle F$

$\frac{a}{d} = \frac{b}{e} = \frac{c}{f}$

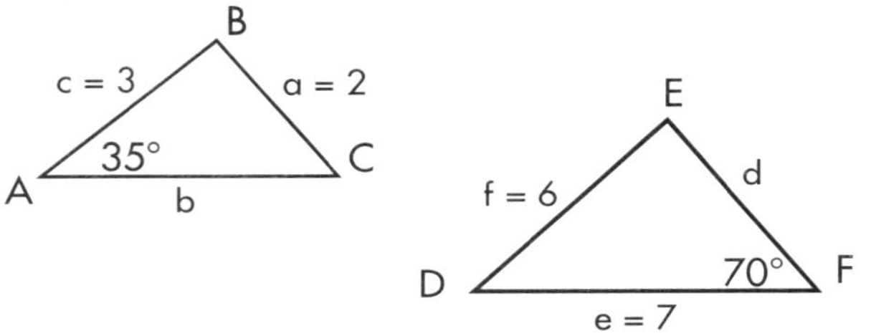

Find the measures of the remaining angles.

Since $m\angle A = 35°$, $m\angle D = 35°$.

We know $m\angle F = m\angle C = 70°$.

Therefore, $m\angle E = m\angle B =$
$180 - (35 + 70) = 75°$.

Find the lengths of the remaining sides.

First, use $\frac{a}{d} = \frac{c}{f}$: $\frac{2}{d} = \frac{3}{6}$

$12 = 3d \rightarrow 4 = d$

Then use $\frac{b}{e} = \frac{c}{f}$: $\frac{b}{7} = \frac{3}{6}$

$6b = 21 \rightarrow b = 3.5$

Directions: For each pair of triangles, $\triangle ABC \sim \triangle DEF$. Write the missing side lengths and angle measurements on every triangle.

1.

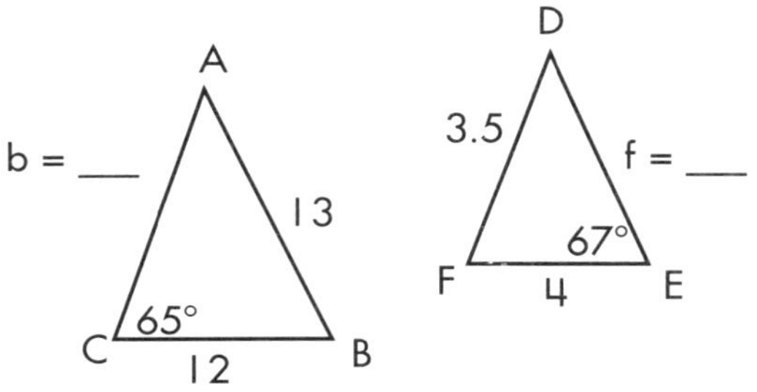

3.

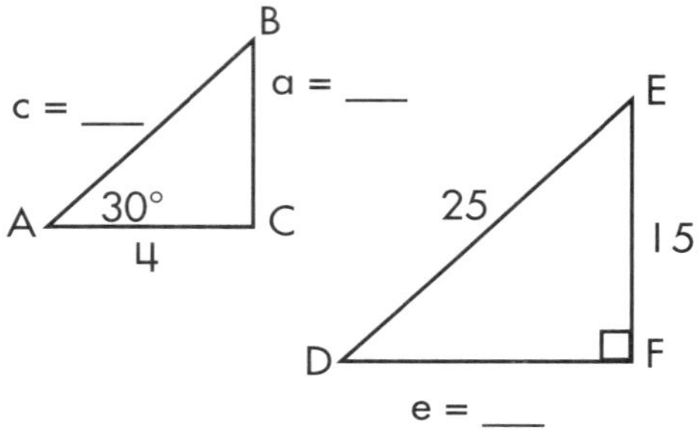

2.

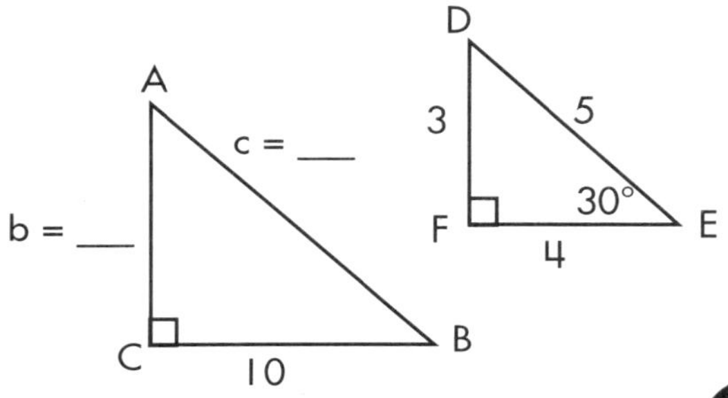

4.

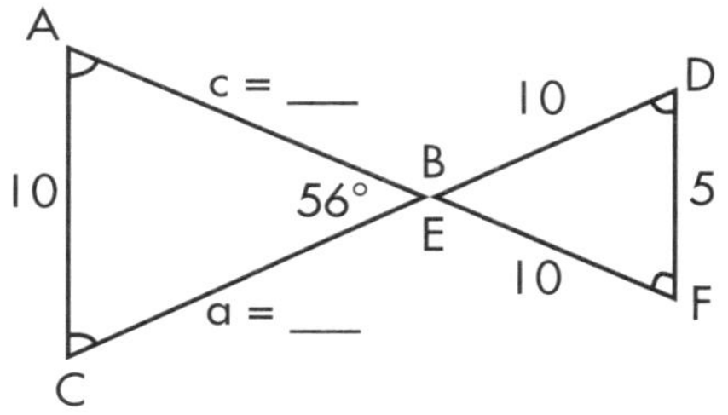

0-7696-4038-9 *Problem Solving*

Name ______________________ Date ___________

Line and Rotational Symmetry

Materials needed: tracing paper

Directions: What types of symmetry does this shape have? Follow the directions below to find out.

1. Find the center of the shape. Draw a vertical and a horizontal dotted line through the center of the shape. Then trace the shape onto tracing paper.

2. Flip your tracing paper over the vertical dotted line. Does the traced image match up with the original shape? _________ Flip your tracing paper over the horizontal dotted line. Does the traced image match up with the original shape? _________

3. Does the shape have a vertical or horizontal line of symmetry? How do you know?

4. Does the shape have any other lines of symmetry? Describe the process you use to find out.

0-7696-4038-9 *Problem Solving*

Name ____________________ Date __________

Line and Rotational Symmetry (cont.)

5. Place the traced image over the original image. Draw a star along the vertical line above the traced image. Then find the center of the shape. Place your pencil at the center of the image. Rotate the traced image clockwise while keeping the original shape still. Keep rotating until the traced image matches up with the original shape. Do the figures match up before you rotate the traced image in one complete circle? __________

6. Answering yes to problem 5 means the shape has rotational symmetry. When describing rotational symmetry, it is important to know the angle of rotation. Continue to turn the traced image. Keep track of how many times it matches up with the original shape during one complete circle.

a. How many degrees are in a complete circle? __________

b. How many times did the traced image match up with the original shape? __________

c. What is the angle of rotation for one turn of the traced image? __________
Show your work.

7. How can transformations help you analyze a shape for symmetry?

EXTENDING

Draw two shapes, one with line and rotational symmetry and one with just line symmetry. Exchange your drawings with a classmate. Discuss which ones have which type of symmetry.

Name ______________________ Date ___________

Coordinate Grid Transformations

Directions: Plot each of the given points to create and compare triangle movement.

1. Draw a triangle with vertices A ($^{-}2$, 2), B (3, $^{-}4$), and C ($^{-}1$, $^{-}2$).

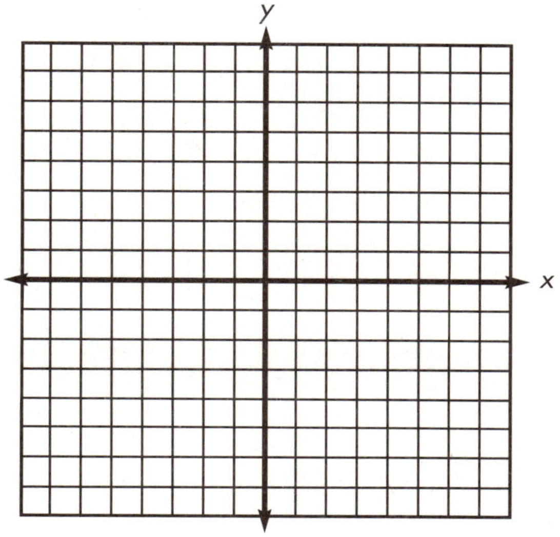

2. Add 3 to each *x*-coordinate of △ABC and draw △DEF.
D (___,___), E (___,___), F (___,___)

3. Compare △ABC and △DEF. ______________________________

4. Add $^{-}4$ to each *x*-coordinate of △ABC and draw △GHI.
G (___,___), H (___,___), I (___,___)

5. Compare △ABC and △GHI. ______________________________

6. Add 3 to each *y*-coordinate of △ABC and draw △JKL.
J (___,___), K (___,___), L (___,___)

7. Compare △ABC and △JKL. ______________________________

8. Add $^{-}4$ to each *y*-coordinate of △ABC and draw △MNO.
M (___,___), N (___,___), O (___,___)

9. Compare △ABC and △MNO. ______________________________

0-7696-4038-9 *Problem Solving*

Name ____________________ Date __________

More Transformations

A **transformation** is a rule for moving a figure to a new location. **Slides** (translations), **turns** (rotations), and **flips** (reflections) maintain the figure size.

Directions: Use the grids to show the indicated transformations. Label corresponding points.

1. Slide 3 units right and 2 units down.

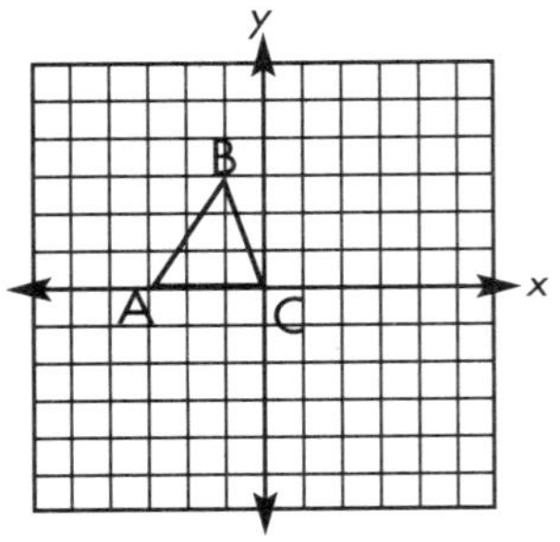

2. Turn 90° clockwise about P.

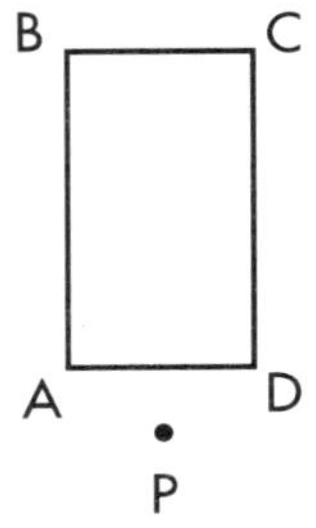

3. Flip over the *y*-axis.

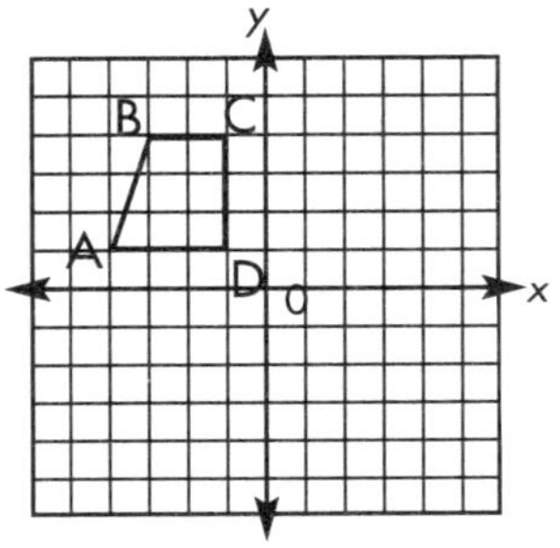

4. Slide 6 units left and 4 units up.

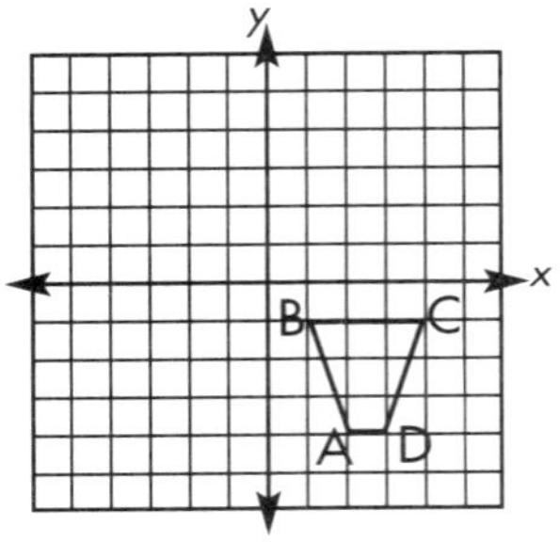

5. Turn 180° counterclockwise about P.

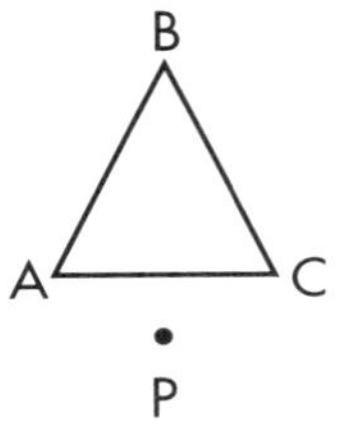

6. Flip over the *x*-axis.

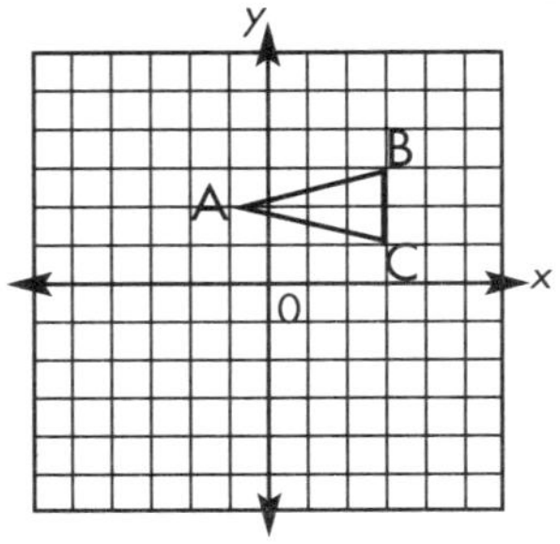

0-7696-4038-9 *Problem Solving*

Name ______________________ Date ____________

Check Your Skills–Geometry

1. If $\overline{MN} \parallel \overline{RS}$, $\overline{MO} \parallel \overline{NR} \parallel \overline{QS}$, $\overline{OR} \parallel \overline{MS} \parallel \overline{NQ}$, $m\angle NMP = 75°$, $m\angle RPS = 40°$, find the following angle measures. Then explain how you know your answers are correct. Use correct vocabulary terms in your explanation.

a. $m\angle MNP$ = __________

b. $m\angle MPO$ = __________

c. $m\angle RPS$ = __________

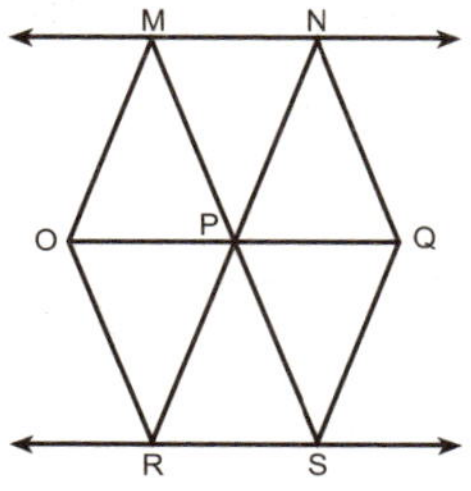

2. On the circle, identify a tangent, radius, chord, semicircle, and minor arc. Use each term's definition to support your answers.

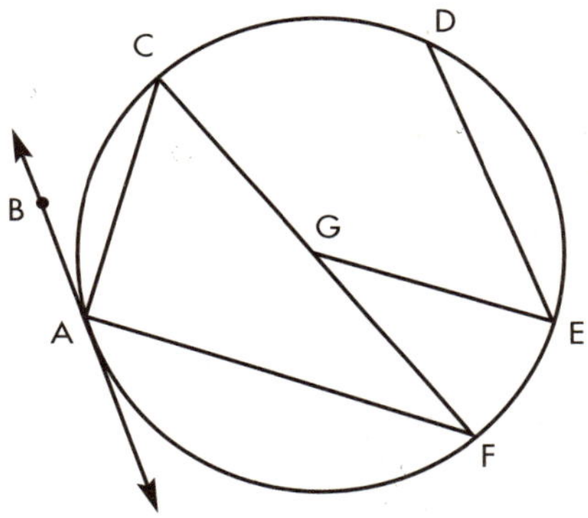

3. Marcus is building a triangular tool shed with the dimensions below. Explain to Marcus whether his plans will work. Give two reasons to support your answer.

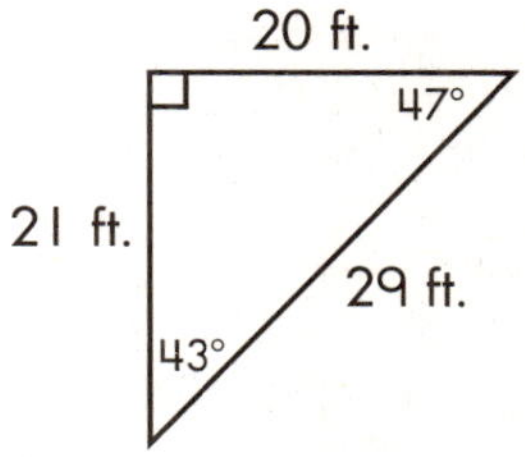

4. Brennan draws a cylinder with a radius of 5 cm and a height of 10 cm. Dray draws a cube with a side length of 9.25 cm. Which shape has the larger volume? Explain how you know your answer is correct.

Name ____________________ Date __________

Area of a Trapezoid

Directions: Answer the questions to help you find the area of the trapezoid.

A trapezoid has two bases, b_1 and b_2, and a height, h. Think of a trapezoid as being made up of a rectangle and 2 triangles. Answer the questions below to figure out how to find the area of a trapezoid.

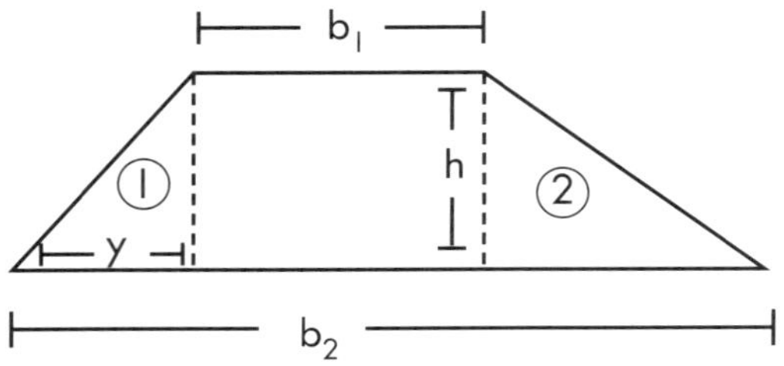

1. How do you find the area of a rectangle?

2. Write an expression that calculates the area of the rectangle.

3. How do you find the area of a triangle?

4. Examine triangle 1, which has a base length of y. Write an expression that calculates the area of triangle 1.

5. Consider the situation where $b_1 = 5$, $b_2 = 8$, $h = 4$, and $y = 2$. What is the length of the base of triangle 2? Write a number sentence to show how you found your answer.

6. Write an expression that calculates the length of the base of triangle 2.

Name ____________________ Date ____________

Area of a Trapezoid (cont.)

7. Write an expression that calculates the area of triangle 2.

8. Write an equation that calculates the area of the entire trapezoid.

9. Simplify your equation as much as possible. Show your work.

10. Write a formula for finding the area of a trapezoid if you know the lengths of the 2 bases, b_1 and b_2, and the height, h.

11. Find the area of the trapezoid where $b_1 = 6$, $b_2 = 10$, and $h = 4$. Show all of your work.

12. Find the area of the trapezoid where $b_1 = 3$, $b_2 = 6$, and $h = 2$. Show all of your work.

EXPLAINING

Describe the process you used to find a formula for the area of a trapezoid.

Name ______________________ Date ___________

Volume of Prisms and Pyramids

Directions: Pete's Party Supplies sells a box of confetti shaped like a rectangular prism with the measurements shown in the sketch here. How much confetti does the container hold? Respond to the following items to find out.

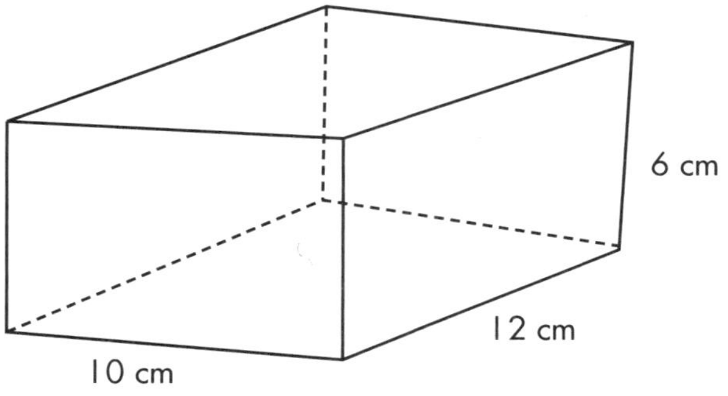

1. Think of a 1-cm thick layer of confetti at the bottom of the box. How much confetti would cover the bottom surface? Show your work, identify any formulas, and describe the type of measurement you found.

2. How many of these layers of confetti would it take to fill the box? __________

3. How much total confetti is in the box? Describe all of the steps it takes to find the amount of confetti in the box. What type of measurement is this?

4. Explain how to find the amount of confetti in a box with a base length of l, a base width of w, and a height of h cm.

Name ____________________ Date __________

Volume of Prisms and Pyramids (cont.)

Pete has come up with a clever new marketing scheme to take advantage of a new trend of Egyptian-themed parties in his area. He is going to put his confetti into a container shaped like a rectangular pyramid. He chooses to use the same dimensions in the pyramid that he used in the box. Imagine that the pyramid was created by digging out part of the rectangular prism.

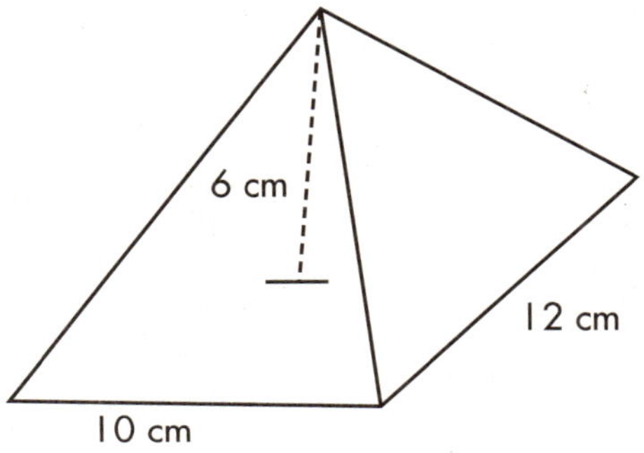

5. Digging out the pyramid divides the prism into how many equal parts? __________

6. Compared to the prism, what fraction of the confetti will the pyramid-shaped container hold? __________

7. Find out how much confetti the pyramid-shaped container will hold. Show your work.

8. Explain how to find the amount of confetti in a pyramid with a base length of *l*, a base width of *w*, and a height of *h* cm.

EXTENDING

Write formulas for finding the volumes of a rectangular prism and pyramid.

Name ____________________ Date __________

Measurement in Context

Directions: Solve each measurement-related question. Show your work so you can prove your answers are correct.

1. Bonnie is planning to carry a rectangular poster at a demonstration. She has the choice of poster board in two sizes. The larger poster board has dimensions of 56 cm by 76 cm. The smaller poster board has dimensions of 35 cm by 50 cm.

a. How many more square centimeters of area per side does the larger poster offer?

b. The larger poster board is priced at $3.89, while the smaller poster board is priced at $2.89. Which board represents a better cost per square centimeter?

2. A box with dimensions of 18 in. by 18 in. by 24 in. is full of loose plastic packing material shaped like peanuts.

a. Would a cylindrical container that is 26 in. tall with a radius of 8 in. be large enough to hold all of the packing material? Explain.

b. What is the difference in volume between the two containers?

3. Jamal is buying a group of solar power panels. He knows that a minimum of 24 sq. ft. of panels are needed for generating the power he needs. The panels come in two sizes: 18 in. by 30 in. and 24 in. by 36 in.

a. If he buys the smaller-size panels, how many will he need?

b. If he buys the larger-size panels, how many will he need?

c. The smaller panels cost $42.89 each, and the larger panels cost $71.20 each. Which size offers the better deal per square foot?

4. Griffin took a storage box with a height of 20 in. and cut off a 4-in. strip all the way around, reducing the height of the box. If the box could hold 2,000 cu. in. of material before the strip was removed, how much can it hold now?

0-7696-4038-9 *Problem Solving*

Name ________________________ Date ____________

Scale Factors

Directions: Solve each proportion problem. Draw a diagram to help you visualize the figures.

1. The following square prisms are similar, with a scale factor of 1:3.

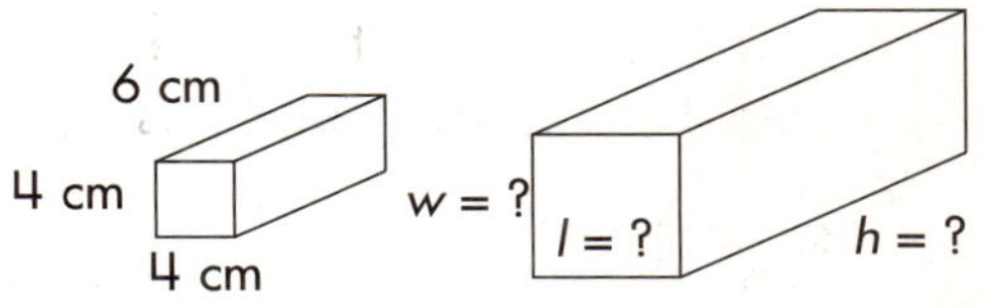

a. $w =$ ________ $l =$ ________ $h =$ ________

b. volume of small prism = ________

c. volume of large prism = ________

d. When the scale factor is 1:3, the volume of the large prism is ________ times greater than the volume of the small prism.

2. The following triangular pyramids are similar, with a scale factor of 1:4.

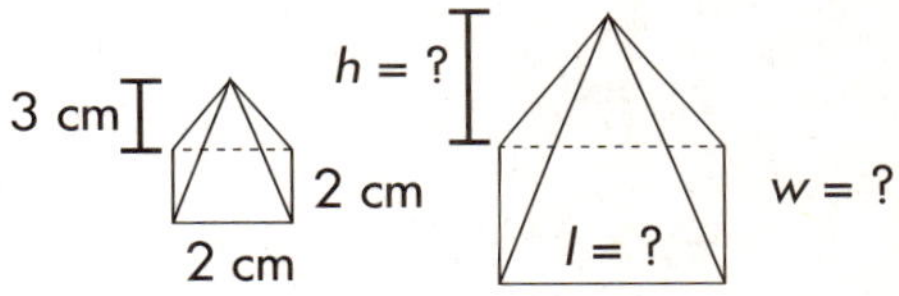

a. $w =$ ________ $l =$ ________ $h =$ ________

b. volume of small pyramid = ________

c. volume of large pyramid = ________

d. When the scale factor is 1:4, the volume of the large pyramid is ________ times greater than the area of the small pyramid.

3. On a separate piece of paper, sketch and label the radius and height of two similar cylinders with a scale factor of 1:5. Find their volumes and then complete the statement below. When the scale factor is 1:5, the volume of the large cylinder is ________ times greater than the volume of the small cylinder.

Look for patterns in your results from problems 1–3 to help answer the following questions.

4. When the scale factor of two similar figures is 1:*k*, the volume of the large figure is ________ times greater than the volume of the small figure.

5. Two hexagonal prisms are similar, with a scale factor of 1:15. The volume of the small hexagonal prism is 8 cm^3. The volume of the large hexagonal prism is ________ .

6. Two spheres are similar, with a scale factor of 1:8. The volume of the small sphere is 10 cm^3. The volume of the large sphere is ________ .

Name ____________________ Date ____________

Scale Factors in Context

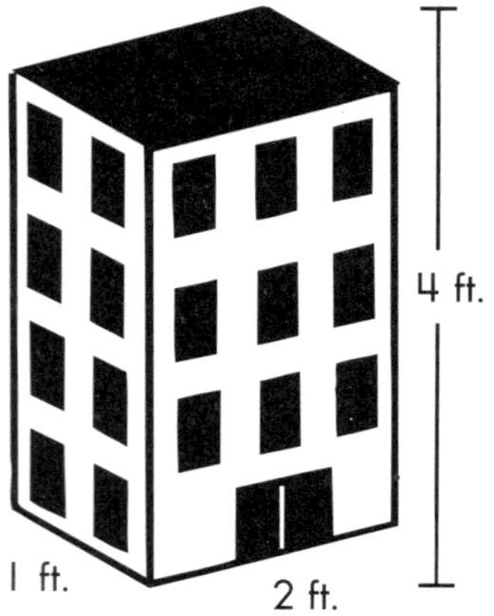

Directions: A scale model of a building shaped like a rectangular prism stands 2 ft. long, 1 ft. wide, and 4 ft. tall.

1. The building is to be built on a scale of $\frac{20}{1}$ with its model.

a. What are the dimensions of the building? ________

b. The outer walls of the building will be made of brick. How many square feet of brick should be bought?

____

c. What is the volume of the building? ________

2. It turns out more space was needed than originally thought. The scale factor is changed to $\frac{25}{1}$.

a. What are the dimensions of the actual building? ________

b. The outer walls of the building will be made of brick. How many square feet of brick should be bought? ________

c. What is the volume of the building? ________

3. Architects are examining the results of using different scale factors to build the actual building. Answer each question below. Then write equations to show the relationships between the scale factor, k, and the measurements of the actual building.

a. How will the dimensions of the building compare to those of the scale model?

$h =$ ________ $w =$ ________ $l =$ ________

b. How will the area of the building's walls compare to that of the scale model?

$A =$ ________

c. How will the volume of the building compare to that of the scale model?

$V =$ ________

Name ____________________ Date __________

Metric Measures

Below are three basic units in the metric system.

The **meter** is the basic unit measure of **length**.
The **liter** is the basic unit measure of liquid **capacity**.
The **gram** is the basic unit measure of **mass**.

The basic unit of meters is frequently expressed in terms of kilometers (1,000 meters) and, for smaller measure, centimeters ($\frac{1}{100}$ of a meter).

Liters are often expressed in terms of milliliters, which are $\frac{1}{1,000}$ of a liter.

The basic unit of grams is often expressed in terms of kilograms (1,000 grams) and, for smaller measure, milligrams ($\frac{1}{1,000}$ of a gram).

Directions: For each of the situations below, state the most appropriate metric measure.

1. The length of a pencil __________
2. The weight of a medium-sized dog __________
3. The amount a water cooler will hold __________
4. A small dose of cough syrup __________
5. The distance between two cities __________
6. The weight of a letter being sent airmail from a foreign country __________
7. The amount of fuel a car's gas tank will hold __________
8. The weight of a hummingbird __________
9. The height of a small child __________
10. The weight of a block of cheese __________

0-7696-4038-9 *Problem Solving*

Name ____________________ Date __________

Metric Measures (cont.)

For each of the sentences below, supply the conversion needed to make a true statement. Show your work to prove your answers are correct.

11. 75 kilometers = _________ meters

12. 500 grams = _________ kilogram

13. 300 meters = _________ kilometer

14. 2,000 milliliters = ________ liter

15. 750 milligrams = ________ gram

16. A 2.6-kilometer hike would be _________ meters.

17. A length of rope 375 cm might be more appropriately expressed as _________ m.

18. A 2-L quantity of olive oil will be divided equally among 4 friends into _________ mL amounts.

19. A large pepperoni sausage 1.2 m in length will cut into 4 equal pieces of _________ cm each.

20. A large block of butter weighing 3,200 g is _________ kg.

21. Twenty pieces of licorice each measuring 20 cm would stretch _________ m if laid end to end.

REFLECTING

Why do you think the metric system is the preferred measurement system for scientific applications?

0-7696-4038-9 *Problem Solving*

Name ____________________ Date __________

Conversions

Directions: For each of the problems, calculate the necessary conversions to find the answer. Show your work and explain how you know your answers are correct.

1. Merrick was tired of all of the snow. On Monday it snowed 32 in. On Tuesday 25 cm fell. Wednesday brought one foot of snow. On Thursday a meter of snow covered the already immense piles of snow. Friday concluded the school week with 10 in. of new snow.

a. How many meters of snow fell from Monday through Friday?

b. What was the average daily snowfall in inches?

2. LaKeisha works for a very particular client who wants his lawn edged every week for the entire summer. LaKeisha measures the rectangular lawn and finds that it is 25 yd. wide and 36 yd. deep. If she walks around the edge of this lawn every day for 13 weeks, what portion of a mile will LaKeisha have walked?

3. Mindy's Mean Marshmallow Marvels contain 2 lbs. of graham crackers, 18 oz. of chocolate, 10 oz. of marshmallows, and 6 oz. of nuts for a recipe that serves 10 people. A friend asks Mindy to cater an anniversary party and requests that she bring enough of her dessert to serve 120 guests. How many pounds of each of the ingredients will Mindy need?

4. A giraffe weighs about $\frac{1}{5}$ times as much as an African elephant. An African elephant weighs about 6,000,000 g. About how many kilograms does a giraffe weigh? Explain your thinking.

0-7696-4038-9 *Problem Solving*

Name ______________________ Date __________

More Conversions

Directions: For each of the problems, calculate the necessary conversions to find the answer. Show your work and explain how you know your answers are correct.

1. A black-bellied hamster weighs about $8\frac{1}{8}$ times more than a golden hamster. A golden hamster weighs about 112,000 mg. About how many grams does the black-bellied hamster weigh? Explain your thinking.

2. Last week Nancy ran three times, running a total of 45.59 km. On Monday she went to the track and ran eight 1,500 m. On Wednesday she ran 10,000 m along the beach. How many kilometers did she run on Saturday? Explain how you found your answer.

3. An ant was trying to get back to his anthill that was 29 cm away. He would walk 10 cm toward his anthill. However, the wind was so strong that he would be blown backward 20 mm. If he kept walking at this rate, how many centimeters would he have traveled in total when he reached his anthill?

4. Susan and Steve are driving to work together when Susan notices that the speedometer is not working. Unfortunately, they don't have time to stop and get it fixed. To get to work on time, they have to maintain a speed of 55 mph. If there is a clock in the car and if Steve knows that the stripes in the broken line on the road are six feet long with six feet of space between the stripes, how can he calculate the car's speed? What will the car's optimum speed be if it is expressed in the units with which Steve is using to calculate the car's speed?

0-7696-4038-9 *Problem Solving*

Name ______________________ Date __________

Rates

Directions: Calculate the necessary conversions to find each answer. Show your work.

1. Nadine's bicycle wheels are rotating at a rate of 3.23 revolutions per second. Her tires have a diameter of 26 in. At this rate, how many miles will she travel in an hour? Show your work.

2. In Michigan, gas costs $2.99 (in U.S. dollars) per gallon. Mrs. Turner travels to Canada, where gas costs $0.66 (in CAN dollars) per liter. The exchange rate is $1.25 Canadian for every $1 U.S. There are approximately 3.78 liters in every gallon of gas. Should she fill up her minivan before or after crossing the border into Canada? Show your work.

3. A truck has tires with a diameter of 16 in. The truck is traveling at 60 mph. How many times do the wheels have to rotate per second to get the truck to move at that speed? Show your work.

4. Noah's new foreign car can travel 12.7 km per liter of gas. This sounds like a lot, but Noah has difficulty thinking in terms of kilometers and liters. He needs to know how many miles the car can travel on a gallon of gas. There are approximately 1.6 km in a mile. Show your work.

REFLECTING

Why is it important to pay attention to the units when solving these problems?

0-7696-4038-9 *Problem Solving*

Name ______________________ Date __________

Check Your Skills—Measurement

1. Find the perimeter and area of the following curved shape. Include the appropriate units in your answer. Explain how you found the measurements.

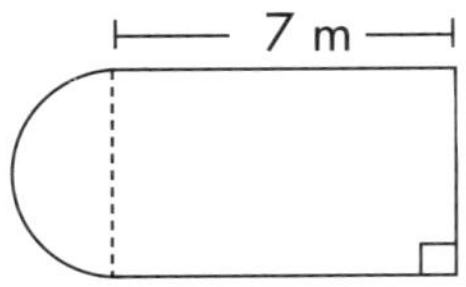

2. Compare the surface area and volume for the following rectangular prism. Which one is the larger measurement?

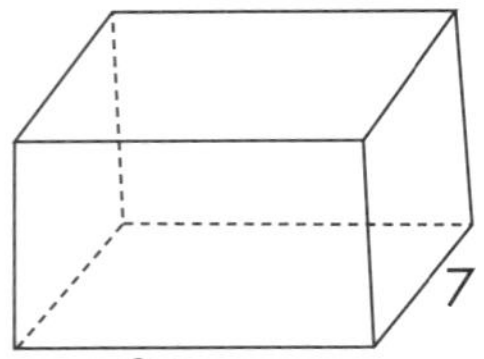

3. The following triangles are similar, with a scale factor of 1:4.

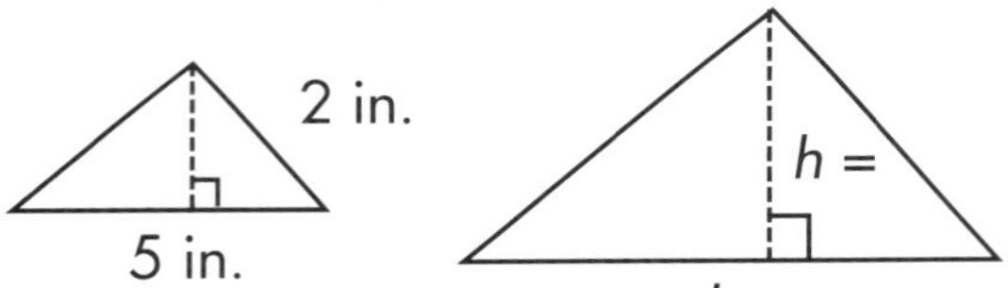

a. Find the measurements and areas of both triangles.

b. Using the scale factor, the area of the large triangle is how many times greater than the area of the small triangle?

4. Treyvon can climb a rope at a rate of 374 cm/10 sec. How many meters per minute is this? Explain how you arrived at your answer.

0-7696-4038-9 *Problem Solving*

Name ____________________ Date __________

Mean, Median, Mode, and Range

The **mean** (or average) is found by dividing the sum by the number of data values. When the data is arranged in numerical order, the middle one is the **median**. The value that occurs most frequently is the **mode**. The **range** is the difference between the greatest and the least value.

Directions: Mike's test scores in spelling were 94, 88, 72, 90, 70, 89, and 70.

1. What was his mean score? ____________
2. What was his median score? ____________
3. What was his mode score? ____________
4. Which score (mean, median, mode) do you think he would like to see on his report card? Why? ______________________________
5. What was the range of Mike's spelling scores? ____________

The chef at Bistro Café found it challenging to satisfy all of his diners. The ages of the diners one evening were as follows: 87, 58, 54, 61, 3, 35, 31, 28, 3, 16, and 68.

6. What was the mean age? ____________
7. What was the median age? ____________
8. What was the mode? ____________
9. Based on the mean age, what should the chef serve—steak and lobster or macaroni and cheese? ____________
10. Based on the mode age, what should be served? ____________

REFLECTING

How does one outlier affect a set of data's measures?

0-7696-4038-9 *Problem Solving*

Name ______________________ Date __________

Measures of Center and Spread

Directions: A survey was distributed to a random sample of 45 students at Applewood Jr. High School. The students were asked the following question:

How many hours a week do you watch television?

Here is the data that was collected.

30, 42, 30, 2, 35, 36, 12, 37, 30, 20, 31, 20, 35, 25, 35, 26, 13, 20, 30, 30, 12, 33, 0, 25, 30, 35, 8, 30, 25, 23, 35, 20, 37, 35, 3, 15, 20, 36, 8, 18, 30,12, 25, 32, 39

1. Calculate the following measures of center. Explain what each one tells you about the data.

- **a.** Mean: __________
- **b.** Median: __________
- **c.** Mode: __________

2. Calculate the following statistics. Explain what each one tells you about the data.

- **a.** Lower quartile: _______
- **b.** Upper quartile: _______
- **c.** Interquartile range: _______

3. Use a separate piece of graph paper. Display the data in a histogram and a box-and-whiskers plot on the same grid.

4. Look at the graphs. Compare the mean and the median of the data. Which is higher? Why does that make sense based on the shape of the graph?

5. Summarize the data. Be as specific as you can. Include statistics and the shape of the graphs in your summary.

EXPLAINING

Why might it be useful to look at two different types of graphs for the same data set?

Name ____________________ Date __________

Frequency Tables and Histograms

Directions: Fran and Fred Franklin decided to sell some items at a flea market. The Franklins sold 40 items, ranging in price from $1 to $40. As items were bought, they wrote the amounts in a list.

1, 1, 39, 40, 2, 2, 5, 19, 20, 20, 5, 6, 8, 8, 8, 10, 10, 25, 29, 30, 10,
10, 11, 12, 12, 15, 5, 6, 15, 15, 18, 21, 22, 25, 25, 30, 36, 40, 2, 33

Fran and Fred wondered at which price range most items were bought. Fran started to organize the information into a frequency table.

1. Complete Fran's table.

Fran's Frequency Table

Price Intervals	Tally	Frequency
$1–$5		
$6–$10		
$11–$15		
$16–$20	IIII	4
$21–$25		
$26–$30		
$31–$35		
$36–$40		

Fred wanted to see a graph of the information. He started to draw a frequency histogram.

2. Complete his histogram.

Fred's Frequency Histogram

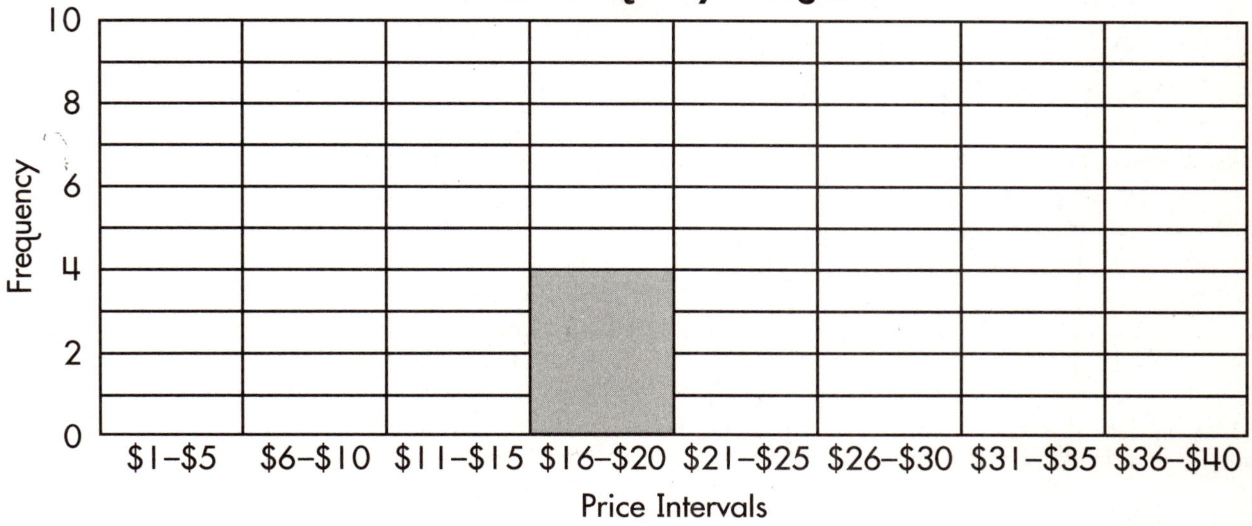

3. In which price ranges were the greatest and least number of items sold? ____________

0-7696-4038-9 *Problem Solving*

Name ______________________ Date __________

Stem-and-Leaf Plots

Directions: Juan and José created this stem-and-leaf plot to compare the amount of money they earned over the summer. Use the stem-and-leaf plot to answer the questions.

Juan Leaf	Stem	José Leaf
9 9 6	0	6 7
8 7 7 5 5 5 5 4 3 3 2 2 2	1	0 0 1 2 3 4 5 5 5 7 8 9
1	2	0 2 5 6
5 0 0	3	1

12 = 2 | 1 | 0 = 10

1. By comparing the medians, who earned the most? Explain your thinking.

____

____

2. By comparing the modes, who earned the least? Explain your answer.

____

____

3. By comparing the means, who earned the most? Justify your thinking.

____

____

____

4. If Juan and José both work approximately 5 hours each day, what would be each person's hourly rate of income? Explain your thinking.

____

____

____

EXTENDING

Graph Juan's and José's information using another representation, such as a scatterplot or a histogram.

Name ____________________ Date __________

Taking a Survey

Directions: Do girls spend more money on themselves than boys? Collect and analyze data to help answer this question.

1. Survey 40 girls and 40 boys. Ask them to write down the amount of money they spend on themselves this week. Record the results of the survey.

2. On a separate piece of graph paper, display the two sets of data in histograms, stem-and-leaf plots, or box plots.

3. Compare the two sets of data. What is similar? What is different?

4. Answer the research question: Do girls spend more money on themselves than boys? Use the data to justify your answer.

EXTENDING

Come up with your own research question involving two different populations in your school. Collect data and display it in a graph. Compare the two groups and answer your research question.

Name ______________________ Date __________

Samples and Populations

Data can be collected in a variety of ways. Polling large numbers of people before an election is an example of collecting data. Recording the types and numbers of birds visiting a backyard bird feeder is another example. Some Web sites, often without people even knowing, gather data about those who visit the sites.

Studying a **sample** enables researchers to make predictions without having to actually study the entire **population**. Sometimes the predictions made about a population are wrong because the information gathered was faulty or did not accurately represent the overall population. In spite of the drawbacks, using a sample provides researchers with a good opportunity to study a larger population.

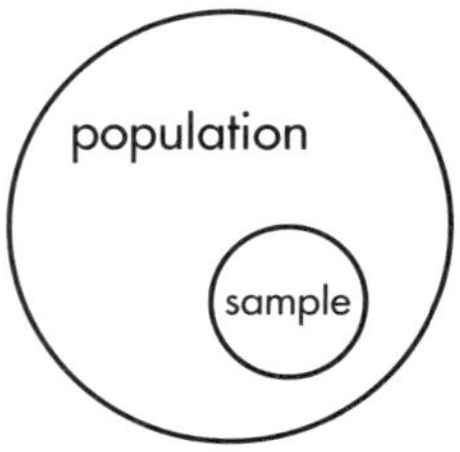

Directions: For each of the samples below, write what the larger population would be. There are many possible correct answers.

1. The students enrolled in Mr. Craven's music class at New Briton elementary school
2. People who voted in the last local election
3. Water samples taken from different locations within a national park
4. People who belong to a trade union in a particular state
5. Radio listeners who listen to talk radio programs during the day

For each of the populations described below, write a smaller sample that could be taken. There are many possible answers.

6. Members of a local health club
7. Scientists who study environmental issues
8. All migrating birds
9. Animals that live year-round in cold-weather environments
10. People who have had a serious illness requiring hospitalization
11. Causes of delays in airline travel

0-7696-4038-9 *Problem Solving*

Name ______________________ Date ____________

Interpreting Data

Directions: Twenty people of the same age in a certain city were randomly selected to take part in a survey. Each person reported his or her education level and annual income. The data in the table shows the results of the survey.

Years of Education	Annual Salary	Years of Education	Annual Salary
10	$18,000	17	$85,000
11	$21,000	18	$71,000
12	$20,000	19	$99,000
13	$48,000	20	$43,000
14	$40,000	20	$140,000
15	$100,000	21	$61,000
16	$40,000	21	$100,000
16	$80,000	22	$240,000
17	$38,000	23	$180,000
17	$50,000	24	$140,000

1. Display the data in a scatterplot. Choose appropriate scales and label your axes.

0-7696-4038-9 *Problem Solving*

Name ______________________ Date ____________

Interpreting Data (cont.)

2. Look at the graph. Describe any patterns you see in the data.

3. Use a ruler and a pencil to draw a line of best fit. In other words, draw a line that is closest to fitting the pattern in the data.

a. Compare your line with those drawn by other classmates. What are the strengths and weaknesses of each line? Whose line do you think fits the data the best?

b. What are some of the characteristics of a line of best fit?

c. Keep trying until you find the line you believe to be the best fit. Clearly draw the line on your scatterplot.

4. Look at the pattern of your line. Describe the pattern in detail. Does the line increase or decrease? How does the rate change?

5. Write an equation to model your line of best fit. Explain how the numbers in the equation relate to the situation.

REFLECTING

How can a line of best fit be useful in a real-life situation?

Name ____________________ Date __________

Using Data to Make Predictions

Interpolation and **extrapolation** are two basic techniques for analyzing data. Both techniques involve using known data to make predictions about the unknown.

Interpolation is the process of making a prediction between known data points.

Extrapolation is the process of making a prediction beyond a known data point.

Example: The Art Function Glass Company is a growing business that specializes in making decorative glass items, window panes, and other functional glass products. The company's sales figures are shown on the scatterplot below. One year's sales figures were not available and, therefore, could not be shown on the scatterplot.

The Art Function Glass Company Sales, 1989 – 1997

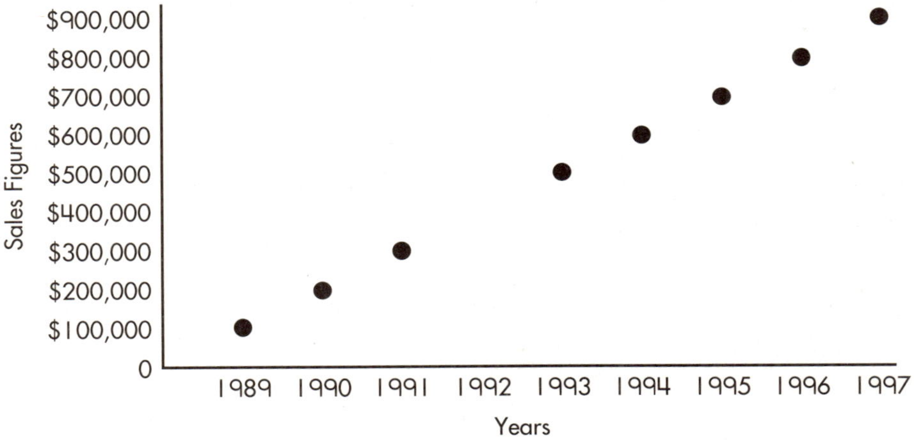

Using Interpolation: What were sales for this company in 1992?

Since there are several years of steadily increasing sales figures prior to 1992 and several more years beyond 1992, a pattern has been revealed by the known data. A likely figure for 1992's sales would be $400,000. However, since the actual 1992 sales figures are not known, the figure of $400,000 cannot be stated with certainty. It is only a prediction that is based on what can be observed in the known data set.

0-7696-4038-9 *Problem Solving*

Name ____________________ Date __________

Using Data to Make Predictions (cont.)

Using Extrapolation: How much money did this company make in sales in 1998?

Sales might have been $1,000,000 in 1998. While the known sales figures for this company do show a steadily increasing trend, it can only be predicted that sales were $1,000,000 in 1998. However, since that information is not shown, it cannot be assumed. 1998 could have been the year that this company tripled sales from the previous year. 1998 might also have been the year that a fire destroyed the factory, thus reducing profits.

Directions: For each of the situations described below, write *interpolation* or *extrapolation* in the blank to denote which technique is being described.

_______________ **1.** A businessperson is trying to predict the new values of properties near a planned amusement park.

_______________ **2.** A stock trader uses prices of stocks over a three-month period to predict tomorrow's closing price of a stock.

_______________ **3.** A researcher makes an important discovery in the laboratory and tries to re-create the experiment by repeating the conditions that led to the discovery.

_______________ **4.** A farmer looks at rainfall data collected over many years and tries to predict how much rain will fall during the upcoming growing season.

_______________ **5.** A researcher tries to determine the past population growth of a historical city over a period of years for which there is only sporadic data available.

_______________ **6.** A wildlife biologist tries to predict the future rate of decline of an animal population based on past and current observations.

_______________ **7.** A person who knows the precise sunrise time for both Monday and Wednesday is trying to calculate Tuesday's sunrise time.

_______________ **8.** A member of the track team has been charting the practice times of team members over a period of weeks, carefully noting their improvement in hopes of predicting their performance at an upcoming track meet.

Name ____________________ Date __________

Probability

The **probability** of an event is the ratio of the number of favorable outcomes to the number of possible outcomes.

Drawing a spade from a deck of cards:

$$P(\text{spade}) = \frac{\text{\# of spades}}{\text{\# of cards}}$$

$$P(\text{spade}) = \frac{13}{52} \text{ or } \frac{1}{4}$$

Choosing a red token from a bag with 6 red, 4 blue, and 5 white tokens:

$$P(\text{red}) = \frac{\text{\# of red}}{\text{\# of tokens}}$$

$$P(\text{red}) = \frac{6}{15} \text{ or } \frac{2}{5}$$

Directions: Calculate the probability ratio of drawing the indicated cards from a deck.

1. P(ace) = ______

2. P(heart) = ______

3. P(black 5) = ______

4. P(red card) = ______

5. P(face card) = ______

6. P(Q of hearts) = ______

For problems 7–12, consider a bag containing 6 red, 4 blue, and 5 white tokens. Calculate the probability ratio of drawing the indicated token(s).

7. P(blue) = ______

8. P(white) = ______

9. P(red or blue) = ______

10. P(not red) = ______

11. P(not blue) = ______

12. P(green) = ______

When only two events can occur and not at the same time, the events are called **complementary events**. The sum of their probabilities is 1.

$$P(\text{even number}) = \frac{3}{6} = \frac{1}{2}$$

$$P(\text{odd number}) = \frac{3}{6} = \frac{1}{2}$$

$\frac{1}{2} + \frac{1}{2} = 1$, complementary

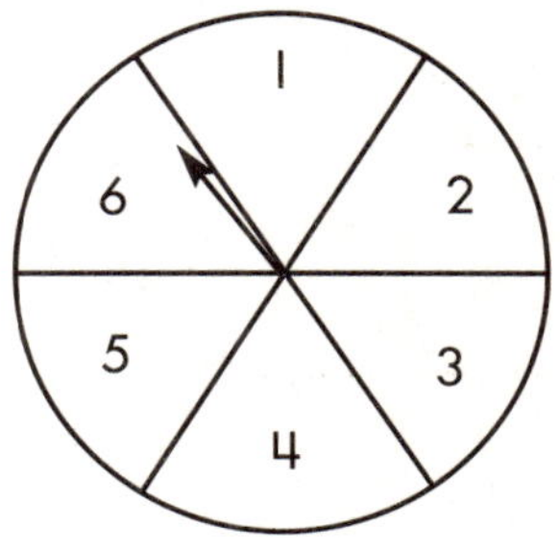

Using the spinner at the right, calculate the probability ratios and state whether the events are complementary.

13. P(# < 3) = _____

P(# > 2) = _____

_____ + _____ = _____

____

14. P(prime) = _____

P(composite) = _____

_____ + _____ = _____

____

15. P(6) = _____

P(≠ 6) = _____

_____ + _____ = _____

____

0-7696-4038-9 *Problem Solving*

Name ______________________ Date __________

More with Probability

Directions: Two brown-eyed people (B) each carry a recessive blue-eyed (b) gene. Only a child with 2 blue-eyed genes (bb) will have blue eyes.

1. Fill in the table below, showing all possible gene combinations a child could receive.

		Dad B	Dad b
Mom	B		
	b		

2. What is the probability that a child of this couple will have blue eyes? __________

3. What happens if they have two children? Complete the following diagram to show all possible genetic combinations of the two children.

1st Child	2nd Child	Eye Colors
BB	BB	brown - brown
	Bb	brown - brown
	bB	brown - brown
	bb	brown - blue
Bb	____	____
	____	____
	____	____
	____	____

1st Child	2nd Child	Eye Colors
bB	____	____
	____	____
	____	____
	____	____
____	____	____
	____	____
	____	____
	____	____

0-7696-4038-9 *Problem Solving*

Name ______________________ Date ____________

More with Probability (cont.)

4. How many total possible genetic combinations are there? Justify your answer.

5. What is the probability that both children will have brown eyes? ________

6. What is the probability that only one child will have blue eyes? ________

7. What is the probability that both children will have blue eyes? ________

8. Describe how you found the probabilities.

9. Explore similar probabilities for hair color. Research dominant and recessive types of hair color. Create a diagram to determine the probability of the different combinations. Interpret the results and explain their meaning.

EXPLAINING

What happens if you find the sum of the probabilities from problems 5–7? Explain why this happens.

0-7696-4038-9 *Problem Solving*

Name ______________________ Date ___________

Check Your Skills—Data Analysis and Probability

1. A recent study by Galloping Polls, Inc., revealed that the mean amount of television watched by Americans is an astonishing 30 hours per week! Which of the sets of data below (showing hours of viewing per week for 10 viewers) would make this number the *most* accurate reflection of people's viewing habits? Justify your answer.

Set 1—70, 70, 70, 10, 10, 8, 4, 18, 5, 40
Set 2—100, 5, 3, 2, 55, 35, 40, 30, 25, 5
Set 3—10, 20, 40, 15, 30, 40, 35, 45, 35, 30

2. Mr. Bundy, the owner of Finest Fashion Shoes, has to put in a new order for his fall shipment of shoes. His assistant has given him a mean, a mode, and a median number for the sizes of shoes sold from the summer order. Which of these numbers do you think would be most important in determining what sizes of shoes Mr. Bundy should order for the fall? Explain your answer.

3. Dante made this graph representing his usual drive to work. What are some possible interpretations of the data that Dante graphed? What realistic explanations might there be for the ups and downs? Explain what you see in the graph.

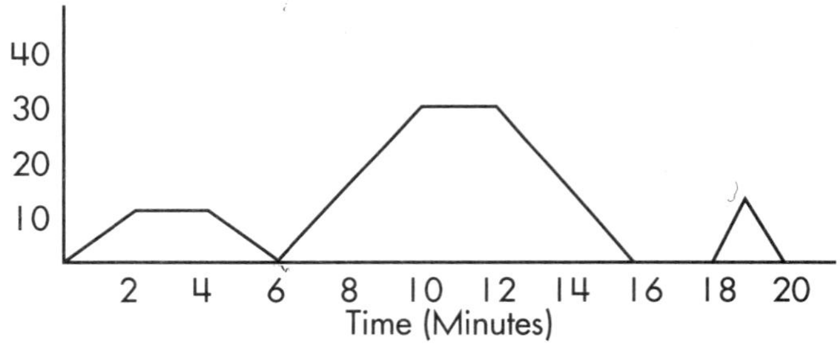

4. Ben likes to garden. Now that spring has arrived, he needs to decide how to arrange the seeds in his garden. He has lettuce, carrots, green pepper, marigold, and zinnia seeds. If he mixes up the packets of seeds and places them facedown on a table, what are the chances he will randomly select:

a. a vegetable? __________

b. two vegetables in two draws? __________

c. a vegetable and a flower in two draws? __________

d. three flowers in three draws? __________

e. three vegetables in three draws? __________

Name ______________________ Date ____________

Cumulative Assessment

1. Which of the following numbers are composite? Explain how you know.

31, 39, 42, 69, 73, 77, 83

2. Luc bought a painting at a charity auction. He spent \$3,060, which was 255% of the actual value of the painting. What was the actual price of the painting? Explain how you know your answer is correct.

3. Sydney wants to take out a one-year used-car loan for \$2,000. Bank One offers an interest rate of 13.99% per year, with no deposit needed. Bank Two offers an interest rate of 15% on one-year used-car loans but needs a \$500 down payment. Compare these two offers and explain to Sydney which one is the better deal.

4. Gerard earns 4% commission on every vehicle he sells. This month he sold 6 vehicles for \$25,000 each. How much commission did Gerard earn this month?

5. On Earth a baseball player can throw a ball 280 feet. On Mars he can throw it 3 times as far as he can on Earth, but on Jupiter he can throw it $\frac{2}{5}$ as far. How far can he throw a ball on Mars? How far can he throw it on Jupiter? Assign variables and solve to find the answer.

6. Describe how you can find the slope and *y*-intercept of a line with the following equation. Without graphing, how can you tell if the line will have a positive or negative slope?

$^{-}2x + y = 5$

7. Simplify the following expressions.

a. $(^{-}8)^2 =$ __________

b. $(^{-}16 + 20)^2 + 6 \div (\sqrt[3]{8}) =$ __________

c. $7.49 \times 10^{-6} =$ __________

0-7696-4038-9 *Problem Solving*

Name ______________________ Date __________

Cumulative Assessment (cont.)

8. A ten-foot ladder is leaning up against the side of a house as shown in the drawing. How far up the house does the ladder reach?

9. If $\overline{MN} \parallel \overline{RS}$, $\overline{MO} \parallel \overline{NR} \parallel \overline{QS}$, $\overline{OR} \parallel \overline{MS} \parallel \overline{NQ}$, $m\angle NMP = 75°$, $m\angle RPS = 40°$, find the following angle measures. Then explain how you know your answers are correct. Use correct vocabulary terms in your explanation.

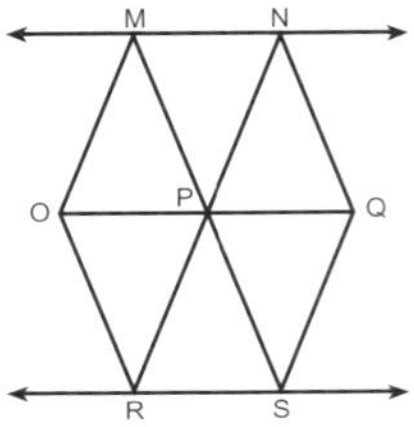

a. $m\angle MNP$ = __________

b. $m\angle MPO$ = __________

c. $m\angle RPS$ = __________

10. The following triangles are similar, with a scale factor of 1:4.

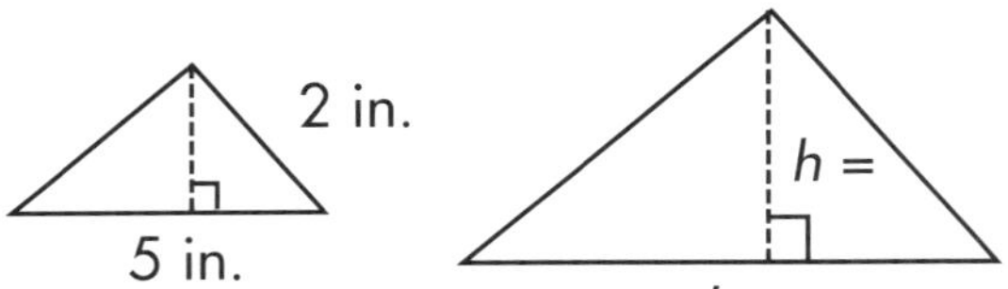

a. Find the measurements and areas of both triangles.

b. Using the scale factor, the area of the large triangle is how many times greater than the area of the small triangle? __________

11. Using the spinner, calculate the probability ratios and state whether the events are complementary.

a. P(# < 3) = __________

P(# > 2) = _____

_____ + _____ = _____

____

b. P(prime) = __________

P(composite) = _____

_____ + _____ = _____

____

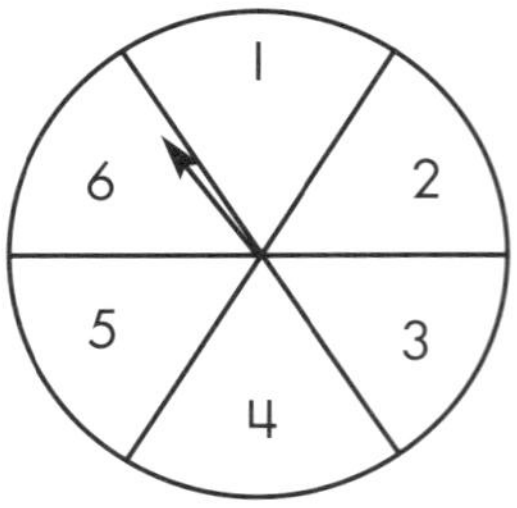

0-7696-4038-9 *Problem Solving*

Answer Key

Pretest **7–8**

1. For both $(^{-}2)^3$ and $(2)^{-3}$, students will find the cube of 2. However a negative exponent takes the reciprocal. So $(^{-}2)^3 = 8$, while $(2)^{-3} = \frac{1}{8}$.
2. **a.** 8.94×10^{10}; **b.** 6.5×10^{-6}
3. 19. Explanations will vary. Students should mention the order of operations.
4. 402,500,000 pairs of tennis shoes
5. Add, then subtract, all odd numbers, alternating signs (+ 3, − 5, + 7, − 9, + 11, − 13, etc.)
6. **a.** $2x = 4 + y$; **b.** *X* more than double *y* equals 6.
7. Marcus's plans will work. The lengths of the walls are accurate per the Pythagorean theorem, and the triangle's angles add up to 180°.
8. tangent: $\overleftrightarrow{AB}$
   radius: $\overline{CG}$ (or $\overline{GE}$, $\overline{GF}$)
   chord: $\overline{AF}$ ($\overline{AC}$, $\overline{CF}$, $\overline{DE}$)
   semicircle: $\overset{\frown}{CDF}$ (or $\overset{\frown}{FAC}$)
   minor arc: $\overset{\frown}{AF}$ (or $\overset{\frown}{CD}$, $\overset{\frown}{FE}$, $\overset{\frown}{ED}$, $\overset{\frown}{AC}$)
9. P = 21.7 m; A = 24.53 m^2; Explanations will vary.
10. Surface area (232 in^2) is the larger measurement.
11. 22.44 m/min.
12. 10, 10, 20, 30, 30, 50
13. **a.** $\frac{1}{8}$; **b.** $\frac{6}{8}$ or $\frac{3}{4}$; **c.** $\frac{4}{8}$ or $\frac{1}{2}$; **d.** $\frac{7}{8}$; **e.** $\frac{6}{8}$ or $\frac{3}{4}$

Types of Numbers **9**

1. **a.** 12, 18, 20, 24, 30; **b.** all even numbers and either a multiple of 6 or 10; **c.** 36, 40, 42
2. 1, 2, 3, 4, 5, 7, 8, 9, 10, 11, 13, 14, 15, 16, 17, 19, 21, 22, 23, 25, 26, 27, 28, 29
3. 6 and 28
4. **a.** 2, 3, 5, 7, 11, 13, 17, 19, 23, 29, 31, 37, 41, 43, 47; **b.** all except the number 1, which has only one factor

Number Explorations **10–11**

1. Treyvon is correct. Examples will vary.
2. Lui is right. The method works for all such numbers.
3. Alicia is not correct. However, numbers with digits that add up to 9 or 18 are always divisible by 9.
4. 15,625; 529; and 4,624 are the perfect squares. Check students' tables and patterns.
5. In order: 8^7; 9^6; 200,000; 11^5; 5×10^4; 8,000; 13^3; 2^{10}; 5^4
6. Multiples of 3 or 11 in the denominator repeat. $\frac{142}{710}$ is the only non-repeating fraction.

Integers and the Commutative Property **12**

1. $^{-}48$, $^{-}40$, $^{-}39$, $^{-}10$, 2, 15, 39, 50
2. $^{-}5{,}472$; $^{-}4{,}560$; $^{-}4{,}559$; $^{-}3{,}201$; $^{-}3{,}021$; $^{-}3{,}012$; $^{-}2{,}999$; $^{-}2{,}891$
3. T
4. T
5. F
6. F
7. T
8. F
9. Yes
10. No; $5 - 3 \neq 3 - 5$
11. Yes
12. No; $6 \div 2 \neq 2 \div 6$

Fractions and the Associative Property **13**

1. H
2. I
3. A
4. E
5. C
6. D
7. $(a + b) + c = a + (b + c)$
8. $a \times (b \times c) = (a \times b) \times c$

Using the Properties **14–15**

1. **a.** 6 x 15; **b.** 15 x 6; **c.** They are equivalent. 6 x 15 = 90, and 15 x 6 = 90. Both result in the same number of CDs; the numbers have just been rearranged; **d.** commutative property of multiplication
2. **a.** 100 + (75 + 60); **b.** (100 + 75) + 60; **c.** They are equivalent. 100 + (75 + 60) = 100 + 135 = 235; (100 + 75) + 60 = 175 + 60 = 235. The total number of jelly beans didn't change even though the groupings changed; **d.** associative property of addition
3. **a.** 4 x 8 + 4 x 10; **b.** 4 x (8 + 10); **c.** They are equivalent. 4 x 8 + 4 x 10 = 32 + 40 = 72; 4 x (8 + 10) = 4 x 18 = 72; The bottles of paint are still the same; they've just been distributed differently; **d.** distributive property of multiplication over addition
4. Answers may vary. One possible solution is given here.
   a. 45 x 23 = 23 x 45, commutative
   b. 17 x (29 + 63) = 17 x 29 + 17 x 63, distributive
   c. (86 + 72) + 211 = 86 + (72 + 211), associative
   d. (7 + 24) x 13 = 7 x 13 + 24 x 13, distributive
   e. 3,456 + 8,192 = 8,192 + 3,456, commutative
   f. 27 x 44 − 18 x 44 = (27 − 18) x 44, distributive

Integers and Exponents **16**

1. 25
2. $^{-}27$
3. $^{-}16$
4. 9
5. $^{-}64$
6. 4,096
7. $\frac{1}{25}$
8. $\frac{1}{27}$
9. $-\frac{1}{125}$
10. $-\frac{1}{32}$
11. $\frac{1}{81}$
12. $\frac{1}{36}$
13. 3
14. 4
15. $^{-}4$

Fractions and Exponents **17**

1. $\frac{25}{36}$
2. $\frac{64}{81}$
3. $\frac{4}{3} = 1\frac{1}{3}$
4. $\frac{81}{100}$
5. $\frac{27}{8}$
6. $\frac{1}{32}$
7. $\frac{9}{8} = 1\frac{1}{8}$
8. $\frac{27}{4} = 6\frac{3}{4}$
9. $\frac{49}{25}$
10. $\frac{3}{4}$
11. No, $(\frac{5}{7})^{-2} = \frac{49}{25}$ or $1\frac{24}{25}$

Answer Key

Scientific Notation

1. **a.** $25{,}000 - 2{,}500 = 22{,}500 = 2.25 \times 10^4$ miles further; **b.** $\frac{2.5 \times 10^4}{2{,}500} = 10$ times as long
2. **a.** $\frac{2{,}500}{50} = 50$ hours from Detroit to San Francisco; **b.** $\frac{25{,}000}{50} = 500$ hours around the equator; **c.** 450 hours longer; **d.** 10 times as long

Squares and Square Roots

1. **a.** It represents the area of the square.
   b. It represents the length of one side of the square.
   c. They are inverse operations. Squaring 3 and then taking the square root of the result will give you 3, which is back to where you started.
2. **a.** $A = 4\text{ cm}^2$; **b.** $A = 12.25\text{ cm}^2$; **c.** $A = 16\text{ cm}^2$
3. **a.** $s = 2.5$ cm; **b.** $s = 4.5$ cm; **c.** $s = 5$ cm
4.

side length (cm)	5	5.5	6.5	7	7.5	9	10.5	11	15.5	18
area (cm^2)	25	30.25	42.25	49	56.25	81	110.25	121	240.25	324

5. Square the length of the side to find the area. $A = s^2$
6. Take the square root of the area of a square to find the length of its sides. $s = \sqrt{A}$

Radicals

1. **a.** $\sqrt{45}$ **b.** $3 \times 3 \times 5$ **c.** $3\sqrt{5}$
2. **a.** $\sqrt{200}$ **b.** $2 \times 2 \times 2 \times 5 \times 5$ **c.** $10\sqrt{2}$
3. **a.** $\sqrt{180}$ **b.** $2 \times 2 \times 3 \times 3 \times 5$ **c.** $6\sqrt{5}$
4. **a.** $\sqrt[3]{40}$ **b.** $2 \times 2 \times 2 \times 5$ **c.** $2\sqrt[3]{5}$
5. **a.** $\sqrt[3]{54}$ **b.** $2 \times 3 \times 3 \times 3$ **c.** $3\sqrt[3]{2}$
6. **a.** $\sqrt[3]{375}$ **b.** $3 \times 5 \times 5 \times 5$ **c.** $5\sqrt[3]{3}$

Order of Operations

1. 91
2. 26
3. correct
4. 60
5. correct
6. $^{-}1$
7. 5
8. correct

Ratios

1. 9 cups of flour
2. 120 people
3. 3 feet
4. 4:1
5. 3 teenagers
6. 24 inches by 16 inches

Scale

Measurements may vary slightly.

1. 2.3 cm: 92 km
2. 2 cm: 80 km
3. 1.2 cm: 48 km
4. 2.7 cm: 108 km
5. 2.9 cm: 116 km
6. 2.1 cm: 84 km
7. 3.1 cm: 124 km
8. ~1 cm x ~1 cm: 40 km x 40 km
9. $\frac{1}{6}$ in.
10. $\frac{1}{2}$ in.
11. $\frac{5}{8}$ in.
12. 1 in.
13. $\frac{1}{8}$ in.
14. $\frac{3}{8}$ in.

Extending: No, the scale dimensions would be $7\frac{1}{2}" \times 12\frac{1}{2}"$.

Scale Factor

1. 1,776 ft.; 1776 is the year the United States declared its independence.
2. 1.858 ft. x 592 = 1,100 ft.
3. 400 ft. ÷ 592 = $\frac{25}{37}$ ft. = 0.675 ft.
4. 276 ft. ÷ 592 = $\frac{69}{148}$ ft. = 0.466 ft.
5. 3.38 ft. x 592 = 2,000 ft.

Percentages over 100

1. **a.** 108%; **b.** 1.08; **c.** 1.08 x \$65 = \$70.20
2. **a.** 2.50; **b.** 2.5 times greater; **c.** 450,000,000 x 2.5 = 1,125,000,000 units
3. 325%; 3.25 x 80 people = 260 people

Sales Tax

1. \$150
2. \$2.38
3. \$8.04
4. \$0.04
5. \$4,125
6. \$0.77
7. \$46.71
8. \$2,835
9. \$0.13
10. \$1.06

Reflecting: The state with a higher sales tax will probably lose some tax revenue to the state with no sales tax as consumers go there to make purchases, especially on more expensive items.

Commission

1. \$3,000
2. \$2,544.90
3. \$7,400
4. \$45.68

Explaining: This practice would tend to make salespeople less aggressive and more relaxed with customers since their job performance and pay would not be tied so closely to only a sales figure.

Interest

1. \$750
2. \$48.40
3. \$479.80
4. \$20,300
5. Yes

Financial Math in Context

1. \$1,125.29
2. \$240
3. \$4,000,000
4. Option 3 is the most valuable option, worth \$937.50. Option 1 is worth \$750.00, and Option 2 is worth \$712.50.

0-7696-4038-9 *Problem Solving*

Answer Key

1. Examples of properties (commutative, associative, distributive) will vary.
2. **a.** 64; **b.** 19; **c.** 0.00000749
3. For both $(^-2)^3$ and $(2)^{-3}$, students will find the cube of 2. However a negative exponent takes the reciprocal. So $(^-2)^3 = {}^-8$, while $(2)^{-3} = \frac{1}{8}$.
4. 96 feet
5. Bank Two has the better offer. With Bank One, Sydney will spend $2,279.80 to repay her loan. After the $500 deposit with Bank Two, she will pay $1,725 to repay her loan. $1,725 + 500 = $2,225. She will pay $54.80 less by going with Bank Two.
6. 402,500,000 pairs of tennis shoes

1. $3,200
2. 150; There are 15 chairs in each of 10 rows.
3. 12 people have only sisters, and 8 have only brothers.

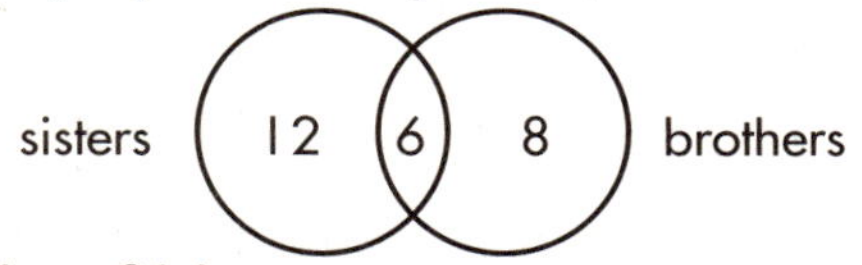

4. about 21 boxes
5. 16 eagles, 24 cougars
6. 158 bottles

1. The race will end in a tie. At the 5-second mark: sixth grader is at 85 yards, seventh grader is at 55 yards, eighth grader is at 25 yards. At the 13-second mark: sixth grader is at 93 yards, seventh grader is at 79 yards, eighth grader is at 65 yards.
2. 10 days
3. Answers will vary. Two 3-pointers and three free throws are impossible given that she scored 32 points.
4. Zach, 37; Zelda, 57; Zany, 70; Zed, 87
5. One box had 57; the other had 38. She needs to find 3 more.

1. 27, 44; Pattern: $y + 5$, $y + 7$
2. 200, 220, 240; Pattern: $y + 20$
3. 106; Pattern: $y \div 2$, $y + 28$
4. 6,561; Pattern: y^2
5. 625; 3,125; Pattern: $5y$
6. 9, 15, 22; Pattern: an addition pattern with each interval increasing by one (+ 1, + 2, + 3, + 4)
7. O, L; Pattern: the alphabet in reverse with every third letter selected
8. triangle, square; Pattern: two triangles, two squares

1. missing members: 8, 13, 21, 34, 55 and 233, 377
2. missing members: 7, 11, 18, 29 and 123, 199
3. Answers will vary, but many of the ratios produced seem to converge to a value of 0.618034.

1. I	**6.** G	**11.** P	**16.** O
2. B	**7.** J	**12.** M	**17.** R
3. A	**8.** H	**13.** L	**18.** Q
4. E	**9.** C	**14.** N	**19.** K
5. D	**10.** F	**15.** S	**20.** T

Check students' tables and graphs.

1. $A = 50 + 8D$; $170 = 50 + 8D$, $D = 15$; Jamel worked 15 days.
2. $D = 15 + 10H$; $47.5 = 15 + 10H$, $H = 3.25$; Emma rode for 3 hours and 15 minutes in the afternoon.
3. $T = 4 + 3G$; $30 = 4 + 3G$, $G = 8.7$; Javier will reach 30 goals during the ninth game.
4. $M = 45N$; $360 = 45N$, $N = 8$; Tanequa's motor scooter has an 8-gallon tank.
5. $W = 100 + 60T$; $725 = 100 + 60T$, $T = 10.4$; It will take Caleb 10.4 minutes to finish writing the paper.
6. $F = 3C$; $135 = 3C$, $C = 45$; There are 45 children at camp on this day.

1. **a.** $C = 0.05p + 0.065p + p = 1.115p$
   b. $269.06
2. **a.** Agency 1: $C = 50 + 0.25m$; Agency 2: $C = 40 + 0.40m$
   b. If you travel 115 miles, agency 1 is the better deal. If you travel 65 miles, agency 2 is the better deal.
   c. Use agency 2 if you plan on traveling less than 66.7 miles. Use agency 1 if you plan on traveling more than 66.7 miles.
3. **a.** Golden Hammer: $C = 0.15p$; Heavy Gavel: $C = 500 + 0.12p$
   b. The commission at Golden Hammer would be $3,750, and at Heavy Gavel it would be $3,500. Heavy Gavel would be the better choice.

1. $x = 31$	**8.** $r = 25$
2. $x = 39$	**9.** $n = {}^-63$
3. $x = 3$	**10.** $a = 44$
4. $x = {}^-19$	**11.** $m = {}^-15$
5. $x = 23$	**12.** $c = 108$
6. $x = {}^-6$	**13.** $f = 8$
7. $y = 35$	**14.** $w = 17$

Extending: son = 13; Juanita = 35; mother = 65

Answer Key

Solving Equations: Scrambled Steps **43**

1. B, D, A, C, E
2. E, B, D, A, C
3. D, C, A, E, B
4. B, A, E, C, D

Functions **44**

1. **a.** 9; **b.** 15
2. **a.** $^-1$; **b.** 2
3. **a.** 2; **b.** $\frac{1}{2}$
4. **a.** $\frac{3}{2}$ (or $1\frac{1}{2}$); **b.** $^-6$
5. **a.** 4; **b.** 16
6. **a.** 2; **b.** $\frac{3}{4}$

Linear and Nonlinear Functions **45–46**

1. All of the points in a linear function will fall in a straight line.
2. **a.** nonlinear; **b.** linear; **c.** linear; **d.** nonlinear; **e.** nonlinear; **f.** nonlinear; **g.** linear; **h.** linear
3. They all have the form $y = mx + b$, where m and b are real numbers.
4. They have the variable taken to a power greater than 1, or the variable is in the exponent.

Graphs and Relationships **47**

1. F
2. A
3. E
4. B
5. C
6. D

Coordinate Plane Graphing **48–49**

1. (5, 3)
2. (9, 3)
3. (1, 4)
4. (0, 3)
5. L
6. C
7. F
8. J
9. 12 square units
10. (5,2)
11. H, E
12. B, C, J
13. No, the points appear scattered and unrelated.
14. Probably not beyond the general conclusion that some of the people in this neighborhood have bought products in the past. The points do not appear to represent a particular pattern or concentration.
15. A pattern of robberies has occurred in this neighborhood, specifically involving convenience stores. An astute detective would want to pay close attention to the fact that a single store has not yet been robbed.

The Equation of a Line **50–51**

1. 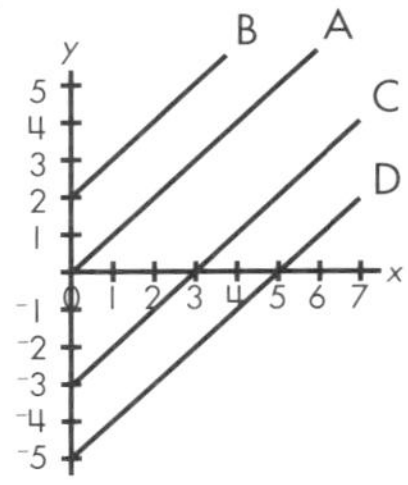

Tables may vary. Check to make sure the points work in the equation.
2. They are all parallel. They all increase at the same rate (up 1, over 1).
3. They all have different y-intercepts.
4. All of the equations add a number to x.
5. The number added to x is different. The number added to x is the place where the graph crosses the y-axis.
6. 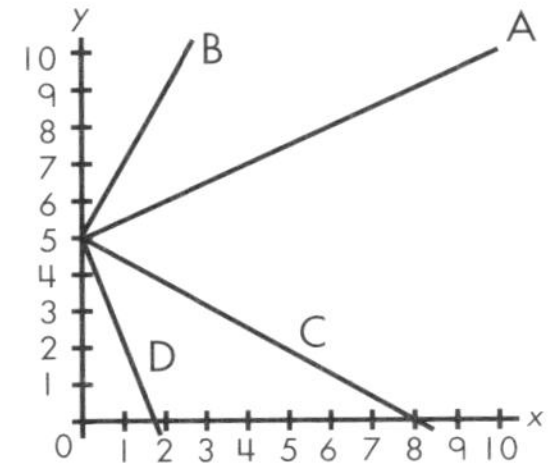

7. They all cross the y-axis at the same point.
8. Two of the graphs increase, and two decrease. They all change at different rates and have different slants.
9. They all have the number 5 added to a term with x in it.
10. A different number is multiplied by x in each equation.

Linear Equations: Finding Intercepts **52**

1.

x	y
0	2
3	0

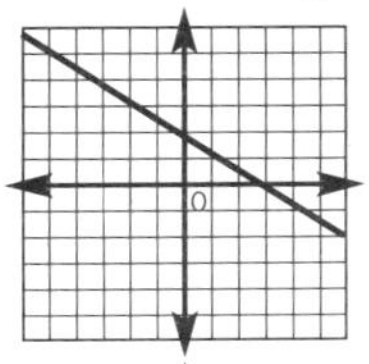

2.

x	y
0	$^-1$
5	0

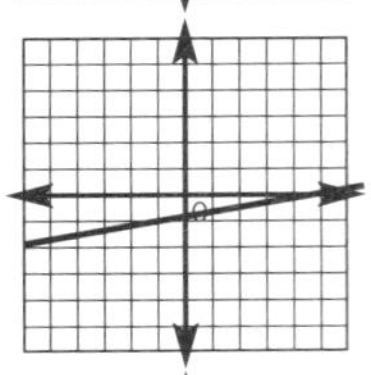

3.

x	y
0	$^-4$
$^-1$	0

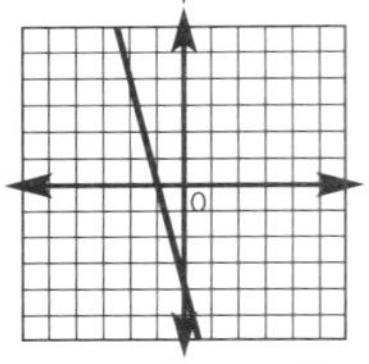

4.

x	y
0	2
$^-5$	0

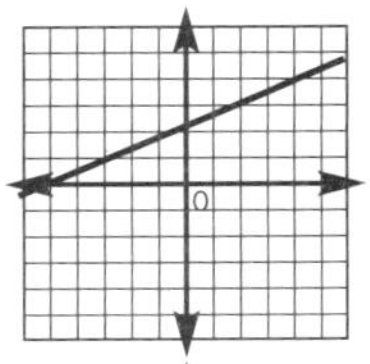

5.

x	y
0	3
$^-3$	0

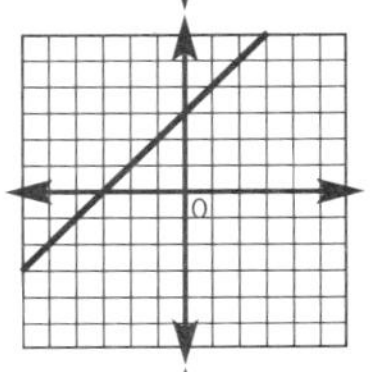

6.

x	y
0	3
1	0

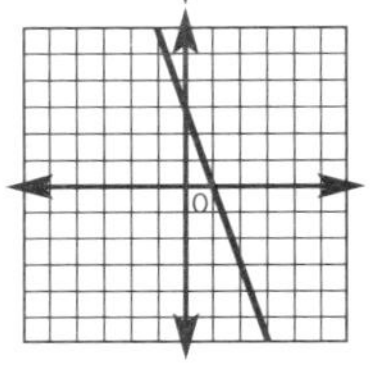

Linear Equations: Slope-Intercept Form **53**

1. 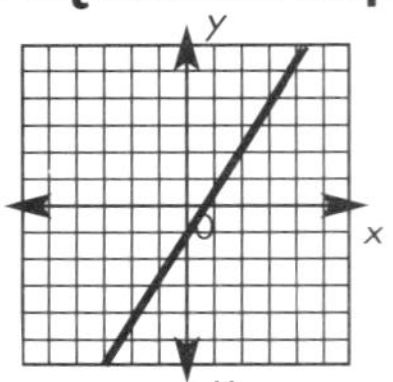
2. 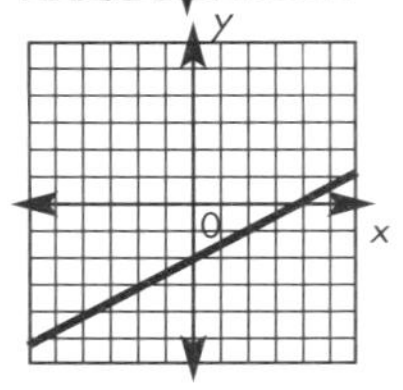
3. 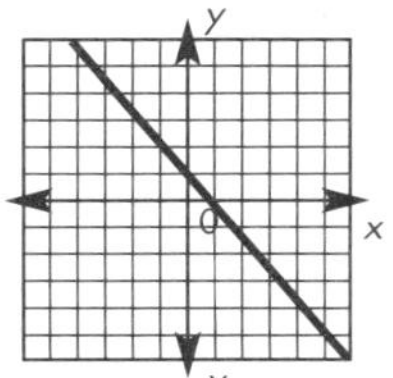
4. 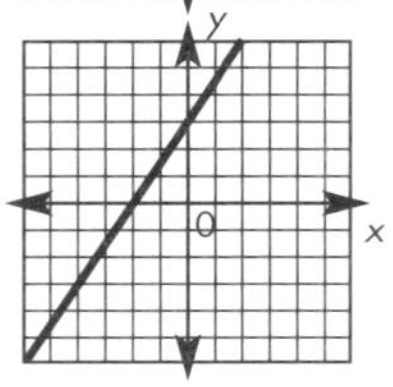

Graphing Linear Equations **54**

1. E, O
2. H, J
3. A, K
4. D, N
5. B, P
6. F, M
7. C, L
8. G, I

Answer Key

Parallel and Perpendicular Lines **55**

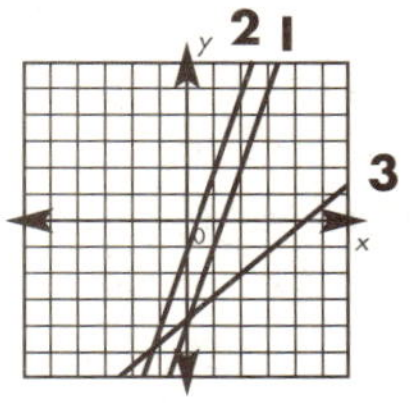

4. Equations 1 and 2 have the same slope. The lines are parallel.
5. Equations 1 and 3 have the same *y*-intercept. The lines are perpendicular.

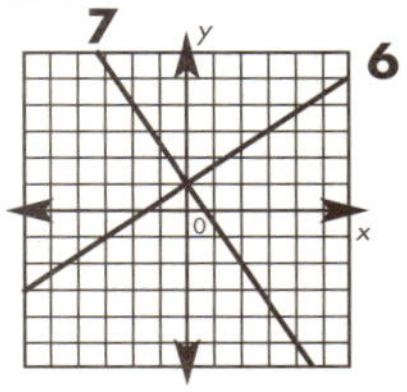

8. Lines 6 and 7 are perpendicular.
9. The slopes of graphs 6 and 7 are opposite reciprocals.

Check Your Skills—Algebra **56**

1. She will buy it on Friday when the sale price is \$13.61.
2. Add, then subtract, all odd numbers, alternating signs (+ 3, − 5, + 7, − 9, + 11, − 13, etc.)
3. E = number of feet on Earth, M = number of feet on Mars, J = number of feet on Jupiter; $M = 3E$; $M = 3 \times 280 = 840$ feet; $J = \frac{2}{5}E$; $J = \frac{2}{5} \times 280 = 112$ feet; on Mars the ball is thrown 840 ft., and on Jupiter it is thrown 112 ft.
4. Answers will vary. Students should put the equation into slope-intercept form ($y = 2x + 5$). From there, students can see that the slope is 2 and the *y*-intercept is 5. Since 2 is a positive number, the slope will be positive and slant from the bottom left quadrant to the upper right quadrant when graphed. The *y*-intercept is the point at which the line will cross the *x*-axis (0, 5).

Classifying Angles **57**

1. **a.** ∠1, ∠2, ∠3, ∠5, ∠8; **b.** ∠4, ∠6; **c.** ∠7, ∠9
2. ∠3 and ∠4, ∠4 and ∠5, ∠5 and ∠6, ∠6 and ∠3, ∠7 and ∠9
3. supplementary pair (straight line or linear pair are also acceptable)
4. 58°
5. 18°
6. 15°
7. 35°
8. 39°
9. 40°
10. ∠13 = 30°, ∠12= 150°
11. 43°; 137°
12. 12°; 102°
13. 45°; 45°

Mixed Practice with Angles **58**

1. g = 23°; h = 67°
2. i = 129°; j = 112°
3. k = 90°; l = 116°; m = 64°; n = 86°
4. o = 13°; p = 78°; q = 91°
5. a = 120°; b = 60°; c = 140°
6. t = 29°; u = 29°
7. v = 39°; w = 59°; x = 121°
8. y = 59°; z = 93°
9. a = 42°; b = 48°; c = 132°
10. a = 60°; b = 50°; c = 80°; d = 100°

Angles and Parallel Lines **59**

1. congruent
2. supplementary
3. congruent
4. congruent
5. congruent
6. **a.** 50°; **b.** 50°; **c.** 130°; **d.** 130°; **e.** 50°; **f.** 50°; **g.** 130°
7. Explanations will vary.
   m ∠1, 3, 6, 8, 9, 10, 13, and 15 are all 115°.
   m ∠2, 4, 5, 7, 11, 12, and 14 are all 65°.

More Angles and Parallel Lines **60**

1. **a.** 40°; **b.** 90°; **c.** 50°; **d.** 40°; **e.** 140°; **f.** 40°; **g.** 40°
2. **a.** 130°; **b.** 60°; **c.** 30°; **d.** 90°; **e.** 130°; **f.** 50°; **g.** 60°
3. **a.** 65°; **b.** 40°; **c.** 40°; **d.** 65°; **e.** 75°; **f.** 65°

Parts of a Circle **61**

1. G
2. B
3. G
4. D
5. F
6. C
7. I
8. H
9. E
10. B
11. H
12. J
13. J
14. A
15. F
16. D

Arc to Arcturus **62**

1. 70°
2. 90°
3. 40°
4. 20°
5. 110°
6. 30°
7. 360°
8. about 20°
9. half
10. 80°
11. 24 cm ($\frac{360}{30} \times 2$)
12. $\frac{1}{6}$

A Triangle Formula **63–64**

1–2. Check students' drawings.

3.

Square 1	Square 2	Square 3
1	4	5
4	4	8
9	16	25
36	48	84

4. Area of Square 1 + Area of Square 2 = Area of Square 3
5. **a.** a^2; **b.** b^2; **c.** c^2
6. $a^2 + b^2 = c^2$
7. **a.** $\sqrt{(4^2 + 5^2)} = \sqrt{(16 + 25)} = \sqrt{41} = 6.4$;
   b. $\sqrt{(5^2 - 2^2)} = \sqrt{(25 - 4)} = \sqrt{21} = 4.6$

Extending: Angles add up to more than 180°, and the side lengths aren't possible according to the Pythagorean theorem.

Answer Key

Perimeter and Circumference 65

1. 76 cm
2. $22\frac{1}{2}$ in.
3. 188.4 m
4. $280\frac{2}{3}$ ft.
5. 17.5 in.
6. 39.8 ft.
7. 42 ft.
8. 31.4 ft.

Area 66–67

Check students' drawings.

1. 800 sq. in.
2. 49 sq. in.
3. 10.94 sq. in.
4. 113.04 sq. m
5. 227.74 sq. in.
6. 63.75 sq. in.
7. 125 sq. ft.
8. 40,920 sq. ft.
9. **a.** 4,320 sq. ft.
b. 0.8333%
10. 2,550.47 sq. ft.

Area Challenges 68

1. 421.5 sq. ft.
2. 4,712 sq. yd.
3. Each hexagon has 3 sq. in. of area; total area is 192 sq. in.
4.

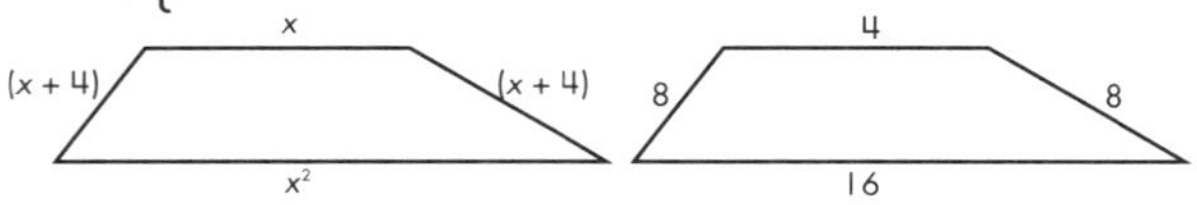

Volume 69–70

1. 108 cu. cm
2. 72 cu. in.
3. 3,140 cu. cm
4. 803.84 cu. cm
5. 768 cu. ft.
6. $V = q^3$
7. $V = \frac{1}{3}y^2h$
8. $V = \pi r^3$
9. $V = (\pi r^2h) - \frac{1}{3}(\pi r^2h)$
10. 1,600 cu. in.
11. rectangular, by 5,538.4 cu. in.
12. 1,402.5 cu. in.

Pyramids and Cones 71

1. Answers will vary but may include $\frac{1}{2}$ for two dimensions, $\frac{1}{3}$ for three dimensions; area—surface, volume—contents
2. 200 cu. ft.
3. 120 cu. ft.
4. 80 cu. ft.
5. 4,312 cu. ft.
6. 66 cu. cm
7. **a.** 480 cu. ft.; **b.** approximately 9 loads
8. **a.** approximately 113.14 cu. cm; **b.** yes

Similar Figures and Perimeter 72

1. P = 18 units
2. P = 9 units
3. a = 6 units
4. ratio = $\frac{3}{10}$
5. P = 9 units
6. ratio = $\frac{2}{7}$

More with Similar Figures 73–74

1. Predictions may vary.
2. Measurements will vary.
3. Measurements will vary.
4. The perimeter of prism 2 will be twice as long as that of prism 1. The surface area of prism 2 will be 4 times as large as that of prism 1. The volume of prism 1 will be 8 times as large as that of prism 1. Explanations may vary.
5. Predictions may vary.
6. **a.** The perimeter of prism 2 will be 3 times that of prism 1. **b.** The surface area of prism 2 will be 9 times that of prism 1. **c.** The volume of prism 2 will be 27 times that of prism 1. **d.** Answers may vary.

Similar Triangles 75

1. 2: d, 4: f, b: $\sqrt{3}$
2. There is no pair of corresponding sides where both measurements are known.
3. **a.** right triangle; **b.** The Pythagorean theorem works for right triangles. The sum of the squares of the legs will be equal to the square of the hypotenuse; **c.** $b = \sqrt{(4^2 - 2^2)} = \sqrt{(16 - 4)} = \sqrt{12} = \sqrt{(4 \times 3)} = 2\sqrt{3}$
4. $2\sqrt{3} : \sqrt{3}$; scale factor = 2:1
5. 2:1 = 4:f, 2 x 2 : 1 x 2 = 4:2, so f = 2; 2:1 = 2:d, so d = 1

Working with Similar Triangles 76

1. $m\angle A = m\angle D = 48°$; $m\angle B = 67°$, $m\angle F = 65°$; b = 10.5, f = 4.3
2. $m\angle A = m\angle D = 60°$; $m\angle B = 30°$; b = 7.5, c = 12.5
3. $m\angle C = 90°$, $m\angle D = 30°$; $m\angle B = m\angle E = 60°$; a = 3, c = 5, e = 20
4. $m\angle A = m\angle D = m\angle F = 62°$; $m\angle E = 56°$; c = a = 20

Line and Rotational Symmetry 77–78

1. Check students' lines and tracings.
2. yes; yes
3. The shape has both vertical and horizontal lines of symmetry. When you flip the traced image over a horizontal or vertical line, the shapes still match up.
4. Yes, the shape has 5 lines of symmetry through the middle of each diamond-shaped peak. Flip the traced image over angled lines, and you will see that the shapes match up.
5. yes
6. **a.** 360°; **b.** 12 times; **c.** 360 ÷ 12 = 30° per rotation
7. Answers will vary.

Coordinate Grid Transformations 79

1.

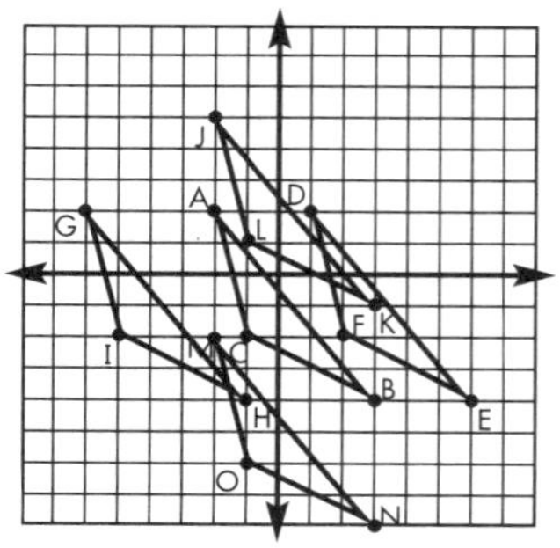

0-7696-4038-9 *Problem Solving*

Answer Key

2. D (1, 2), E (6, ⁻4), F (2, ⁻2)
3. △DEF is △ABC translated 3 units to the right.
4. G (⁻6, 2), H (⁻1, ⁻4), I (⁻5, ⁻2)
5. △GHI is △ABC translated 4 units to the left.
6. J (⁻2, 5), K (3, ⁻1), L (⁻1, 1)
7. △JKL is △ABC translated 3 units upward.
8. M (⁻2, ⁻2), N (3, ⁻8), O (⁻1, ⁻6)
9. △MNO is △ABC translated 4 units downward.

More Transformations 80

1.

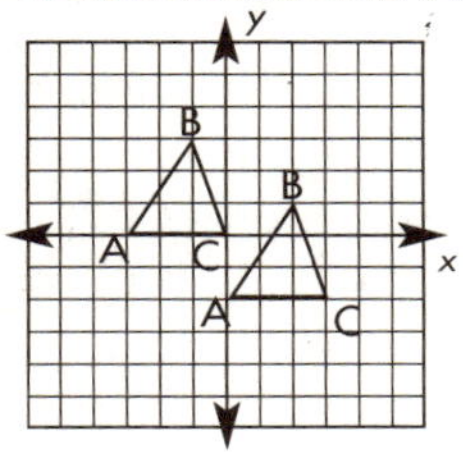

4.

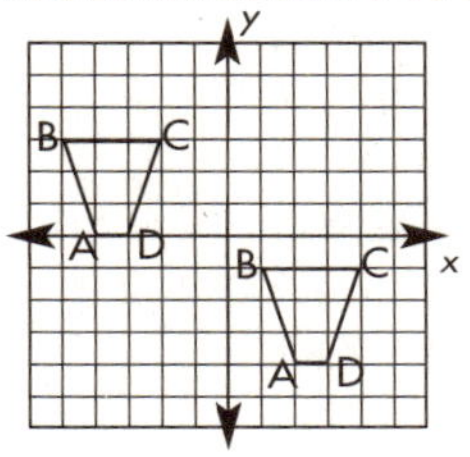

2.

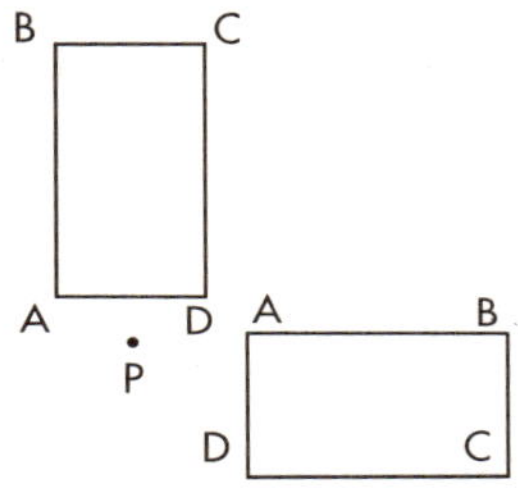

5.

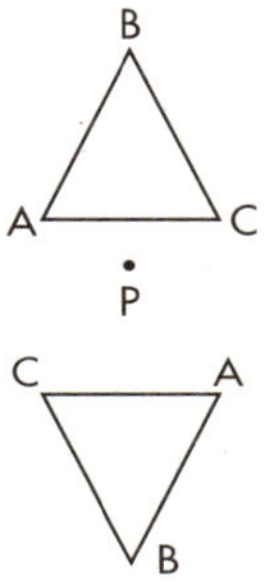

3.

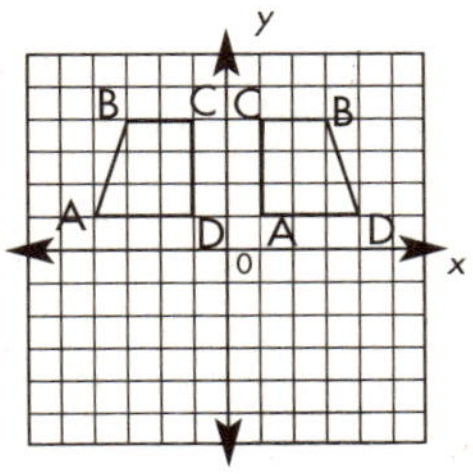

6.

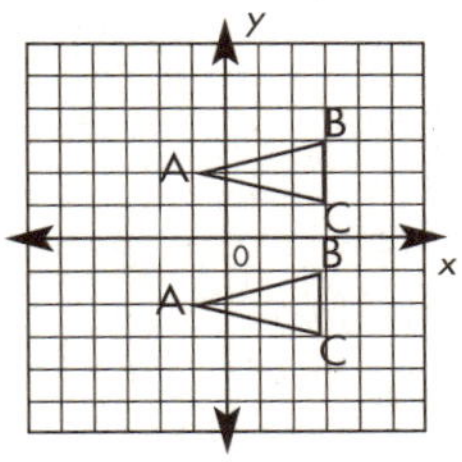

Check Your Skills—Geometry. 81

1. **a.** 65°; **b.** 75°; **c.** 40°; Explanations will vary.
2. tangent: $\overleftrightarrow{AB}$
   radius: $\overline{CG}$ (or $\overline{GE}$, $\overline{GF}$)
   chord: $\overline{AF}$ (or $\overline{AC}$, $\overline{DE}$)
   semicircle: $\overset{\frown}{CDF}$ (or $\overset{\frown}{FAC}$)
   minor arc: $\overset{\frown}{AF}$ (or $\overset{\frown}{CD}$, $\overset{\frown}{FE}$, $\overset{\frown}{ED}$, $\overset{\frown}{AC}$)
3. Marcus's plans will work. The lengths of the walls are accurate per the Pythagorean theorem, and the triangle's angles add up to 180°.
4. The cube has the larger volume. The volume of the cylinder is 785 cm^3, and the cube's volume is 791.45 cm^3.

Area of a Trapezoid 82–83

1. Multiply the base by the height.
2. Area of rectangle = $b_1 \times h$
3. Multiply the base by the height and divide by 2.
4. Area of triangle 1 = $\frac{1}{2}y \times h$
5. $8 - (5 + 2) = 1$
6. length = $b_2 - (b_1 + y)$
7. Area of triangle 2 = $\frac{1}{2}[b_2 - (b_1 + y)] \times h$
8. Area of trapezoid = Area of rectangle + Area of triangle 1 + Area of triangle 2
   $A = b_1h + \frac{1}{2}y\,h + \frac{1}{2}[b_2 - (b_1 + y)]\,h$
9. $A = b_1h + \frac{1}{2}y\,h + \frac{1}{2}[b_2 - b_1 - y] \times h$
   $A = b_1h + \frac{1}{2}y\,h + \frac{1}{2}b_2h - \frac{1}{2}b_1h - \frac{1}{2}yh$
   $A = (b_1h - \frac{1}{2}b_1h) + (\frac{1}{2}yh - \frac{1}{2}yh) + \frac{1}{2}b_2h$
   $A = \frac{1}{2}b_1h + \frac{1}{2}b_2h$
10. $A = \frac{1}{2}(b_1 + b_2) \times h$
11. $A = \frac{1}{2}(6 + 10) \times 4 = \frac{1}{2} \times 16 \times 4 = 32$
12. $A = \frac{1}{2}(3 \times 6) \times 2 = \frac{1}{2} \times 18 \times 2 = 18$

Volume of Prisms and Pyramids 84–85

1. Area of a rectangle = length x width; A = 10 cm x 12 cm = 120 cm^2
2. 6 layers
3. Volume = 120 x 6 = 720 cm^3
4. Find the area of the base, which is a rectangle. So the area will be found by multiplying the length x the width of the base. This will tell you how much confetti covers the bottom of the base. Then multiply the base area by the height (the number of layers of confetti). This will give you the volume of the prism. $V = lwh$
5. 3
6. pyramid = $\frac{1}{3}$ volume of prism
7. $V = \frac{1}{3} \times 720 = 240$ cm^3
8. First, find the volume of the prism with those dimensions (multiply the area of the base times the height). Then multiply the volume by $\frac{1}{3}$ since the pyramid takes up $\frac{1}{3}$ the volume of the prism. $V = \frac{1}{3}lwh$

Measurement in Context 86

1. **a.** 2,506 cm^2; **b.** The larger poster board is the better deal.
2. **a.** No, the box holds 7,776 cu. in. of material. The cylindrical container only holds 5,225 cu. in.; **b.** The box holds 2,551 more cu. in. of material.
3. **a.** 6.4 panels; **b.** 4 panels; **c.** The smaller panels, at $11.44 per square foot, are a better deal than the larger panels, which cost $11.87 per square foot.
4. 1,600 cu. in.

Scale Factors 87

1. **a.** w = 12 cm; l = 12 cm; h = 18 cm; **b.** 96 cm^3; **c.** 2,592 cm^3; **d.** 27

Answer Key

2. **a.** $w = 8$ cm; $l = 8$ cm; $h = 12$ cm; **b.** 4 cm^3; **c.** 256 cm^3; **d.** 64
3. 125
4. k^3
5. 27,000 cm^3
6. 5,120 cm^3

Scale Factors in Context 88

1. **a.** 40 ft. by 20 ft. by 80 ft.; **b.** 8,000 $ft.^2$; **c.** 64,000 $ft.^3$
2. **a.** 50 ft. by 25 ft. by 100 ft.; **b.** 12,500 $ft.^2$; **c.** 125,000 $ft.^3$
3. **a.** The dimensions of the building will be k times bigger than those of the scale model. $h = 4k$; $w = k$; $l = 2k$; **b.** The area of the building walls will be k^2 times bigger than that of the scale model. $A = 20k^2$; **c.** The volume of the building walls will be k^3 times bigger than that of the scale model. $V = 8k^3$

Metric Measures 89–90

1. cm	**8.** mg	**15.** 0.75
2. kg	**9.** cm	**16.** 2,600
3. liters	**10.** g or kg	**17.** 3.75
4. mL	**11.** 75,000	**18.** 500
5. km	**12.** 0.5	**19.** 300
6. g	**13.** 0.3	**20.** 3.2
7. liters	**14.** 2	**21.** 4

Reflecting: The metric system is precise, and the conversions are based on units of ten. Both features make metrics appropriate for scientific applications.

Conversions 91

1. **a.** 2.6 m; **b.** 20.64 in.
2. $\frac{9}{10}$ mi.
3. 24 lbs. of graham crackers, 13.5 lbs. of chocolate, 7.5 lbs. of marshmallows, and 4.5 lbs. of nuts
4. about 1,200 kg

More Conversions 92

1. about 910 g
2. 23.59 km on Saturday
3. 36 cm
4. Speed can be calculated by time and number of stripes passed. The optimum speed is around 403 stripes per minute.

Rates 93

1. Circumference = π x diameter = 3.14 x 26 in. = 81.64 in. The wheel will push the bike 81.64 in. for each revolution. 81.64 in./rev. x 3.23 rev./sec. = 263.70 in./sec. The bike will travel 263.70 inches in a second, or 949,320 inches in an hour (263.70 in./sec. x 3,600 sec./hr. = 949,320 in./hr.). This means the bike will travel 949,320 in./hr. ÷ 12 in./ft. = 79,110 ft./hr. and 79,110 ft./hr. ÷ 5,280 ft./mi. = 14.98 mi./hr. Nadine is traveling 14.98 miles per hour.
2. \$0.66 Canadian dollars per liter x 3.78 liters per gallon = \$2.49 Canadian dollars per gallon; \$2.49 Canadian dollars x 1.25 = \$3.11 U.S. dollars per gallon. Mrs. Turner should fill up on gas while still in Michigan, since \$2.99 a gallon is cheaper than \$3.11 per gallon.
3. 60 mi./hr. x 5,280 ft./mi. = 316,800 ft./hr.; 316,800 ft./hr. x 12 in./ft. = 3,801,600 in./hr.; 3,801,600 in./hr. ÷ 3,600 sec./hr. = 1,056 in./sec.; Circumference of wheel = π x diameter = 3.14 x 16 in. = 50.24 in. The truck moves 50.24 in. for each revolution of the tires. 1,056 in./sec. ÷ 50.24 in./revolution = 21.02 revolutions per second. The truck tires are rotating 21.02 times every second.
4. 12.7 km/L ÷ 1.6 km/mi. = 7.94 mi./L; 7.94 mi./L x 3.78 L/gal. = 30.00 mi./gal. The car can travel 30 miles on a gallon of gas.

Check Your Skills—Measurement. 94

1. P = 21.7 m; A = 24.533 m^2; Explanations will vary.
2. Surface area (232 $in.^2$) is the larger measurement.
3. **a.** base of larger triangle = 20 in.; height of larger triangle = 8 in.; area of small triangle = 5 $in.^2$; area of large triangle = 80 $in.^2$; **b.** 16
4. 22.44 m/min.

Mean, Median, Mode, and Range. 95

1. 81.9
2. 88
3. 70
4. He would want to see his median score since it is the highest.
5. 24
6. 40.36
7. 35
8. 3
9. steak and lobster
10. macaroni and cheese

Measures of Center and Spread 96

1. **a.** mean: 25. The average student watches 25 hours of television a week; **b.** median: 30. Half the students watch 30 or less hours of television a week; **c.** mode: 30. More students watch 30 hours of television than any other amount.
2. **a.** lower quartile: 20. 25% of the students watch 20 or fewer hours of television a week.; **b.** upper quartile: 35. 75% of the students watch 35 or fewer hours of television a week; **c.** interquartile range: The amount of television that 50% of the students watch varies by a difference of 15 hours. Also, 50% of the students watch between 20 and 35 hours of television a week.

Answer Key

3.

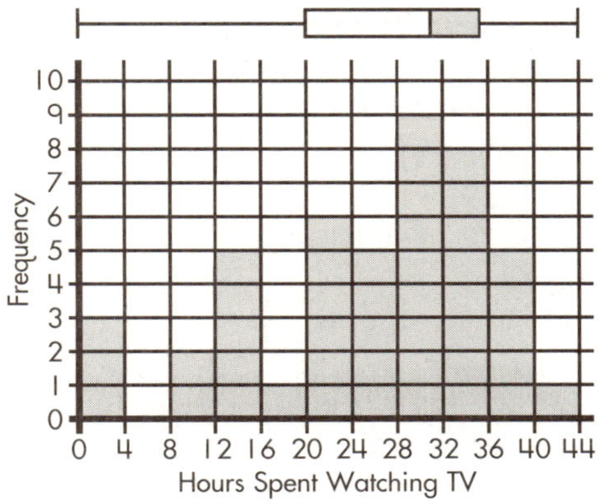

4. The mean is lower than the median. This makes sense because the data is skewed to the left. Half of the students watch 30 or more hours of television a week, but the average amount (25 hours) is lower than that because one student doesn't watch television at all.
5. The data is skewed to the left. Students watch an average of 25 hours of television a week, but 50% of them watch 30 or more hours a week. Twenty-five percent of the students watch 20 hours or less. Twenty-five percent of the students watch more than 35 hours of television a week. One student did not watch television at all, and no students watched between 4 and 7 hours of television a week. Half of the students watched between 20 and 35 hours of television a week.

Frequency Tables and Histograms 97

1. **Fran's Frequency Table**

Distribution of Flea Market Items		
Price Intervals	**Tally**	**Frequency**
\$1–\$5	~~IIII~~ III	8
\$6–\$10	~~IIII~~ IIII	9
\$11–\$15	~~IIII~~ I	6
\$16–\$20	IIII	4
\$21–\$25	~~IIII~~	5
\$26–\$30	III	3
\$31–\$35	I	1
\$36–\$40	IIII	4

2. **Fred's Frequency Histogram**

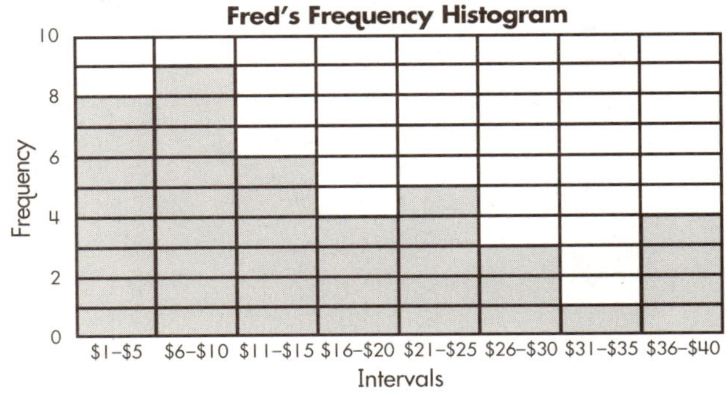

3. greatest: \$6–\$10; least: \$31–\$35

Stem-and-Leaf Plots 98

1. Neither. Their medians are both \$15.
2. Neither. Their modes are both \$15.
3. José (\$16.10 vs. \$16.40)
4. Juan = \$3.28; José = \$3.22

Taking a Survey. 99

Survey results will vary.

Samples and Populations. 100

Answers will vary, but suggestions are provided below.

1. All students enrolled at New Briton Elementary School
2. All people who voted in any of the last 20 local elections
3. Water samples taken from all national parks
4. All people who belong to the same trade union regardless of the state they live in
5. Radio listeners who have listened to any radio program day or night
6. Members of a local health club who use the swimming pool
7. Scientists who study environmental issues and work only for private companies
8. Crows only
9. Polar bears
10. People who have been hospitalized for a stroke
11. Bad weather

Interpreting Data 101–102

1.

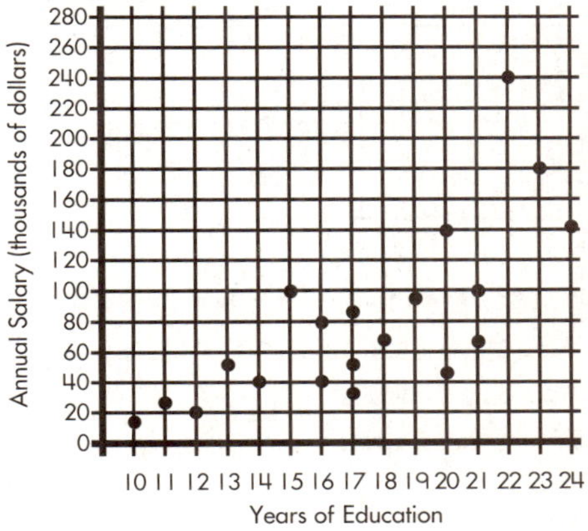

2. As the number of years of education increases, the annual salary increases.
3. Lines may vary somewhat.
   a. Comparisons will vary; **b.** The amount of error between the points and the line should be minimized; **c.** Each student's line may be slightly different. Make sure it's a good estimate of the line of best fit.
4. For each additional year of education, the annual salary increases by about \$10,000. The *y*-intercept of $^-90$ would hypothetically mean that a person with 0 years of education would lose \$90,000 a year. This doesn't make sense. The model should be used only for realistic values. So the *y*-intercept helps give us the line that fits the data, but it shouldn't be interpreted literally in terms of the context.

Answer Key

5. $y = {}^{-}90 + 10x$; The line increases about $10,000 per year.

Using Data to Make Predictions 103–104

1. extrapolation
2. extrapolation
3. interpolation
4. extrapolation
5. interpolation
6. extrapolation
7. interpolation
8. extrapolation

Probability 105

1. $\frac{4}{52}$ or $\frac{1}{13}$
2. $\frac{13}{52}$ or $\frac{1}{4}$
3. $\frac{2}{52}$ or $\frac{1}{26}$
4. $\frac{26}{52}$ or $\frac{1}{2}$
5. $\frac{12}{52}$ or $\frac{3}{13}$
6. $\frac{1}{52}$
7. $\frac{4}{15}$
8. $\frac{5}{15}$ or $\frac{1}{3}$
9. $\frac{10}{15}$ or $\frac{2}{3}$
10. $\frac{9}{15}$ or $\frac{3}{5}$
11. $\frac{11}{15}$
12. $\frac{0}{15}$
13. $\frac{2}{6}$ or $\frac{1}{3}$; $\frac{4}{6}$ or $\frac{2}{3}$; $\frac{1}{3} + \frac{2}{3} = 1$ Complementary
14. $\frac{3}{6}$ or $\frac{1}{2}$; $\frac{2}{6}$ or $\frac{1}{3}$; $\frac{1}{2} + \frac{1}{3} \neq 1$ Not complementary (There are 3 possible outcomes—the number 1 is neither prime nor composite.)
15. $\frac{1}{6}$; $\frac{5}{6}$; $\frac{1}{6} + \frac{5}{6} = 1$ Complementary

More with Probability 106–107

1.

		Dad B	Dad b
Mom	B	BB	Bb
Mom	b	bB	bb

2. $\frac{1}{4}$ or 25%
3.

1st Child	2nd Child	Eye Colors
BB	BB	brown - brown
BB	Bb	brown - brown
BB	bB	brown - brown
BB	bb	brown - blue
Bb	BB	brown - brown
Bb	Bb	brown - brown
Bb	bB	brown - brown
Bb	bb	brown - blue

1st Child	2nd Child	Eye Colors
bB	BB	brown - brown
bB	Bb	brown - brown
bB	bB	brown - brown
bB	bb	brown - blue
bb	BB	blue - brown
bb	Bb	blue - brown
bb	bB	blue - brown
bb	bb	blue - blue

4. 16
5. $\frac{9}{16} = 56.25\%$
6. $\frac{6}{16} = \frac{3}{8} = 37.5\%$
7. $\frac{1}{16} = 6.25\%$
8. number of families with that characteristic ÷ total number of possible combinations
9. Check students' diagrams and explanations.

Check Your Skills—Data Analysis and Probability . . 108

1. Set 3 would be the most accurate reflection.
2. Mode is the measure he should use because he'll want to stock most of the sizes that are most in demand.
3. Answers will vary. Zeros in speed could indicate stop signs, etc.
4. **a.** $\frac{3}{5}$; **b.** $\frac{9}{25}$; **c.** $\frac{12}{25}$; **d.** 0; **e.** $\frac{8}{125}$

Cumulative Assessment 109–110

1. 39, 42, 69, 77; Each of these numbers has factors other than 1 and itself.
2. $1,200 ($3,060 ÷ 255% = $1,200)
3. Bank Two has the better offer. With Bank One, Sydney will spend $2,279.80 to repay her loan. After the $500 deposit with Bank Two, she will pay $1,725 to repay her loan. $1,725 + 500 = $2,225. She will pay $54.80 less by going with Bank Two.
4. $6,000
5. E = number of feet on Earth, M = number of feet on Mars, J = number of feet on Jupiter; $M = 3E$; $M = 3 \times 280 = 840$ feet; $J = \frac{2}{5}E$; $J = \frac{2}{5} \times 280 = 112$ feet; on Mars the ball is thrown 840 ft., and on Jupiter it is thrown 112 ft.
6. Answers will vary. Students should put the equation into slope-intercept form ($y = 2x + 5$). From there, students can see that the slope is 2 and the y-intercept is 5. Since 2 is a positive number, the slope will be positive and slant from the bottom left quadrant to the upper right quadrant when graphed. The y-intercept is the point at which the line will cross the x-axis (0, 5).
7. **a.** 64; **b.** 19; **c.** 0.00000749
8. $\sqrt{51} \approx 7.14$ ft.
9. **a.** 65°; **b.** 75°; **c.** 40°; Explanations will vary.
10. **a.** base of larger triangle = 20 in.; height of larger triangle = 8 in.; area of small triangle = 5 $in.^2$; area of large triangle = 80 $in.^2$
11. **a.** $\frac{2}{6}$ or $\frac{1}{3}$; $\frac{4}{6}$ or $\frac{2}{3}$; $\frac{1}{3} + \frac{2}{3} = 1$ Complementary;
    b. $\frac{3}{6}$ or $\frac{1}{2}$; $\frac{2}{6}$ or $\frac{1}{3}$; $\frac{1}{2} + \frac{1}{3} \neq 1$ Not complementary (There are 3 possible outcomes—the number 1 is neither prime nor composite.)

integer	**prime number**
composite number	**scientific notation**
exponent	**ratio**

0-7696-4038-9 *Problem Solving*

a number that has exactly two factors, 1 and itself

2, 3, 5, 7, 11, 13, 17, 19

any positive or negative whole number and zero

$^{-}13$, $^{-}6$, 0, 24, 178

a way to write very large and very small numbers; written as the product of a number between 1 and 10 and a power of 10

4.5×10^{7} 6.25×10^{-6}

a number that has more than two factors

4, 10, 49, 125, 320

a size comparison of two numbers based on division

2:1 "2 to 1" $\frac{2}{1}$

tells the number of times a number is used as a factor

$4^{③} = 4 \times 4 \times 4$ or 64

variable	**coordinates**
slope-intercept form	**tangent line**
complementary angles	**supplementary angles**

a pair of numbers on a plane, representing one point where the x-axis and *y*-axis meet

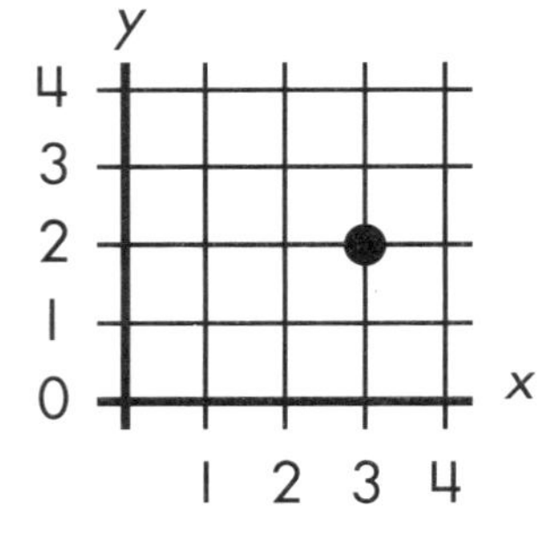

a letter in an expression that represents a quantity that can change

$2b + 5 = 41$

$b = 18$

a line that touches a circle at exactly one point

the equation of a line written in the form *y* = mx + b, where m is the slope and b is the *y*-intercept

$y = 2x - 1$

$y = \frac{3}{4}x - 5$

two angles whose sum is 180°

$105^\circ \angle + 75^\circ \angle = 180^\circ$

two angles whose sum is 90°

$25^\circ \angle + 65^\circ \angle = 90^\circ$

0-7696-4038-9 *Problem Solving*

circumference

perpendicular

parallel

Pythagorean theorem

population

histogram

0-7696-4038-9 *Problem Solving*

lines that meet at a right angle

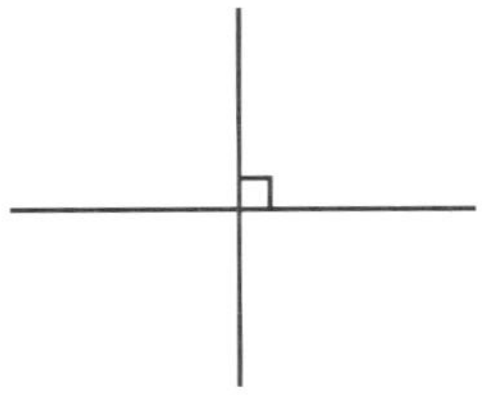

the perimeter of a circle; Circumference = π x diameter

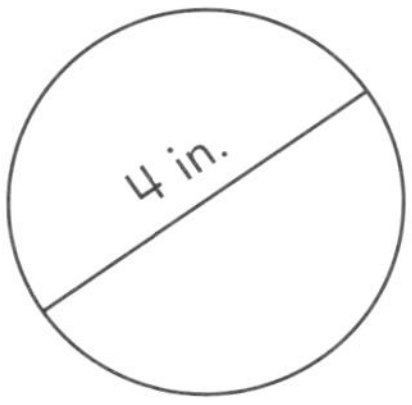

C = π x diameter = 12.56 in.^{2}

the sum of the squares of the lengths of the two legs of a right triangle is equal to the square of the length of the hypotenuse

$a^2 + b^2 = c^2$

$3^2 + 4^2 = 5^2$

lines that do not intersect

a graph that looks similar to a bar graph but displays information in intervals

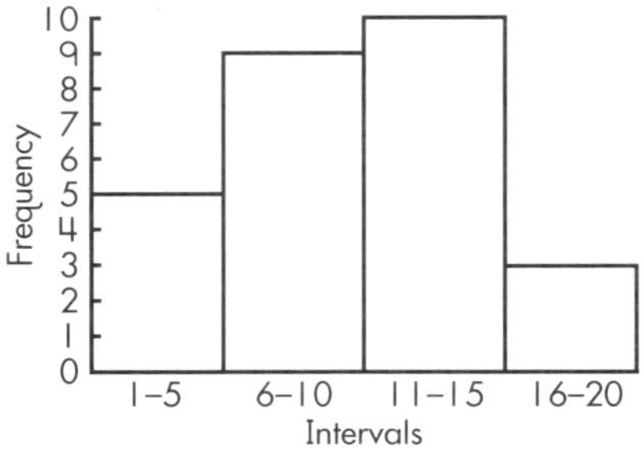

a group of people surveyed for information

small population: fifth graders in a school

large population: everyone living in the United States

0-7696-4038-9 *Problem Solving*

measures of center

range

interpolation

sample

extrapolation

probability

0-7696-4038-9 *Problem Solving*

the difference between the highest value and the lowest value in a group of ordered data

2, 3, 4, 5, 6, 7, 7, 7, 8

8 − 2 = (6)

the mean (average), median (middle), and mode (highest frequency) of a data set

2, 3, 4, 5, 6, 7, 7, 7, 8

mean: 5.4, median: 6, mode: 7

a number of people, objects, or events chosen from a given population to represent the entire group

population: Americans

sample: Americans living in Oregon

the process of making a prediction between known data points

Year 1: 10 units
Year 2: ?
Year 3: 14 units
Year 4: 16 units

interpolation: 12 units

the chance that a given event will occur

$$\frac{\text{number of favorable outcomes}}{\text{number of possible outcomes}}$$

probability of getting "heads" when tossing one coin = $\frac{1}{2}$

the process of making a prediction beyond a known data point

Year 1: 12 units
Year 2: 14 units
Year 3: 16 units
Year 4: ?

extrapolation: 18 units

0-7696-4038-9 *Problem Solving*